Messerschmitt Me 209 V1

David Myhra

Schiffer Military History
Atglen, PA

Sources:
Information in several sections of this book were obtained from Don Berliner's *Victory over the Wind: A History of the Absolute World Air Speed Record*, published by Von Nostrand Reinhold Company, New York, 1983.

Book Design by Ian Robertson.

Printed in China.
ISBN: 0-7643-1107-7

We are interested in hearing from authors with book ideas on military topics.

Published by Schiffer Publishing Ltd.
4880 Lower Valley Road
Atglen, PA 19310 USA
Phone: (610) 593-1777
FAX: (610) 593-2002
E-mail: Schifferbk@aol.com.
Visit our web site at: www.schifferbooks.com
Please write for a free catalog.
This book may be purchased from the publisher.
Please include $3.95 postage.
Try your bookstore first.

In Europe, Schiffer books are distributed by:
Bushwood Books
6 Marksbury Avenue
Kew Gardens
Surrey TW9 4JF
England
Phone: 44 (0)181 392-8585
FAX: 44 (0)181 392-9876
E-mail: Bushwd@aol.com.

Try your bookstore first.

Messerschmitt Me 209 V1

The *Me 209 V1* was the real designation of the air machine which established the Absolute World Air Speed Record for land planes of 469.224 miles per hour [755.138 kilometers per hour] on a *FAI* (*International Aeronautics Federation*) approved 1.86 mile [3 kilometer] long circular course. This record was set on 26 April 1939 at *Messerschmitt AG* facilities near Augsburg by company test pilot *Dipl.-Ing. Fritz Wendel*. *Messerschmitt AG,* as well as *Reich Minister of Propaganda Dr. Josef Goebbels,* had been referring to their record-setting low-wing cantilever monoplane machine in press releases as the *Bf 109R*. Nevertheless, *Messerschmitt's* world air speed record would stand for over thirty years until the American *Darryl Greenamyer*, a *Lockheed* test pilot, set a new piston-engine powered land air speed record of 482.462 mph [776.449 km/h] on 16 August 1969 at Edwards Air Force Base, California. He used a highly modified ex-U.S. Navy, WWII Grumman F8*F-2*, which he had nicknamed the "*Bearcat.*" *Greenamyer's* air speed record would be eclipsed two days short of ten years later on 14 August 1979 by American *Steve Hinton*. He set a new world's record while piloting a highly modified ex-USAAF, WWII North American *Republic P-51 "Mustang.*" Nicknamed the "*Red Baron,*" *Hinton* set the new air speed record for piston-powered aircraft at Tonopah, Nevada, with an average air speed of 499.059 [803.152 km//h]. He bettered *Greenamyer's* ten year old record by 16.597 mph [26.709 km/h] and *Wendel's* forty year old record by only 29.835 mph [48.013 km/h].

The sole reason for the M*e 209V1's* existence was, in fact, to carry out a massive "bluffing," or propaganda, program by the *Reichluftfahrtministerium* (German Ministry of Aviation), or *RLM Technisch Amt* (Technical Office), under the leadership of *Ernst Udet*...the fourth highest scoring ace of WWI with 62 aerial victories. After all, the RLM had selected the *Messerschmitt Bf 109* as their next front-line fighter (replacing the bi-wing *Heinkel He 51*) over the competing *Heinkel He 112*, even though the *He 112*, after numerous modifications, came to be about 50 mph faster than the *Bf 109*. Then, too, although the *He 112* had lost the competition to be Germany's next front line fighter, an all new *Heinkel AG* single fighter prototype designated the *He 100 V2* held two *FAI* Absolute World Air Speed Records: 463.67 mph [746.18 km/h] for the 1.86 mile [3.0 kilometer] course and 394 mph [634 km/h] for the 62 mile [100 kilometer] closed

course. But when it came to a standard, run-of-the-mill *Bf 109E*, its top speed was only 354 mph [570 km/h] at 12,463 feet [3,800 meters]. For the *NAZI Partei*, this would not do. How could *Dr. Josef Goebbels* tell world governments that the *Third Reich's* front-line fighter was the fastest fighter in the world when it didn't even hold a single speed record to prove it? Something had to be done. It appears that during the development stage of the *Bf 109, Ernst Udet* and other high-ranking officers in the *Technisch Amt,* along with *Goebbels*, decided that an aircraft of the *Bf 109* type had to hold the Absolute World Air Speed Record, too. Yet some historians claim that the idea for a record breaking *Bf 109* machine came from *Willy Messerschmitt* himself, and this belief is based on remarks he gave during a lecture at the *German Academy for Aviation Research*:

A ground level view of the Me 209 V1 as seen from its nose, port side. Notice that the machine has no tail wheel, but a spring loaded retractable metal skid, which, when retracted, forms the ventral edge of the rudder. This was done to reduce weight and keep things simple. Scale model and photograph by *Günter Sengfelder***.**

"We need experimental aircraft, indeed, real experimental aircraft in the development of which the designer must be free from all restrictions and considerations imposed by such factors as available tools or the instructions and concepts of a purchaser governed by any practical considerations. The experience gained by a genuine experimental project of this nature will make the development of an aircraft designed to specifications much easier and will ensure greater progress."

But the truth of the matter was that the reputation of *National Socialism* was at stake. Ever since *Adolf Hitler* had come into power in the early 1930s, *NAZI* Germany was spending huge sums to prove that their form of government was capable of technical achievements beyond all democratic- and communist-run countries. It was an embarrassment that the *Heinkel He 100 V2* held two world absolute air speed records, and this machine had not even been selected for serial production as a fighter...*Messerschmitt's Bf 109* had been selected instead.

The selection of a new German single seat single engine fighter goes back to the Summer of *1934* when the *RLM's Technisch Amt* announced a competition to design a mono-wing fighter to replace their bi-plane fighter...the *Heinkel He 51.* The *RLM's* request for proposals sought, among other features, the following: Development of a single seat fighter for day and night air operations; single engine; 400 km/h [249 mph] at 6,000 meters [19,685 feet] altitude; and armament either two machine guns with 1,000 rounds per barrel, or one 20 mm machine cannon with 200 rounds.

Over 700 of the bi-wing *He 51* machines had been built and put into service from the time of its introduc-

tion in 1933. It was sent to Spain in July 1936, flown by *Luftwaffe* volunteer pilots in the *Condor Legion* aiding the *Facist* leader of the *Nationalists...General Francisco Franco.* In fact, some 4,500 *Luftwaffe* men and women volunteered. But the *He 51* had a difficult time serving the *Condor Legion* over Spain with its 4,500 hundred volunteer *Luftwaffe* members because the day of the bi- wing was over. This was one of the great lessons for German aviation planners. It came about thanks in large part to the equipment which the USSR had sent to Spain. The Soviets aided the Spanish Loyalists, giving them their *Polikarpov I-15 "Rata,"* or rat. This was their diminutive mono wing fighter with its powerful radial engine, and the *Luftwaffe* discovered that it was a bit too much for their *He 51* bi-wing. Later, *Hitler* sent in a number of *Bf 109s* mainly to test them under front line conditions. The *Facists* won the civil war on 28 March 1939. *Adolf Galland,* who began his career with the *Condor Legion,* was so taken by the *I-15 "Rata"* that when he returned to Germany he persuaded *Kurt Tank,* managing director of *Focke-Wulf,* to design a fighter aircraft prototype with many of the characteristics of the *"Rata."* The result of their

combined input was the *Focke-Wulf Fw 190* fighter of 1941.

The winner of the new fighter competition of 1934 would be pretty much assured of a contract from the *Luftwaffe* for mass producing perhaps as many as 20,000 of these mono-wing machines, it was believed. Actually nearly 40,000 *Bf 109s* would be constructed before Germany's unconditional surrender on 8 May 1945. But in 1934 four companies were in competition...but only two were the competition: *Heinkel* with its *He 112* and *Messerschmitt* with their *Bf 109.* Both had about equal performance with their almost 700 horsepower (take off horsepower) *Jumo 210Ea (Rolls-Royce "Kestrel") Vee* 12 cylinder upright liquid cooled engines, with the *He 112* being about 50 mph [80.5 km/h] faster. Competitors number 3 [*Arado*] and 4 [*Focke-Wulf*] equipped their machines with German-built 600 horsepower (take off horsepower) *Junkers Jumo 210C (Rolls-Royce "Kestral") Vee* 12 cylinder upright liquid cooled engines and were never seriously in the running. *Arado's* entry, its *Ar 80,* even had a fixed landing gear with wheel spats, while *Focke-Wulf's* entry, its *Fw 159,* had a braced parasol wing

A direct port side view of the Me 209 V1. During its record-breaking flights the machine's raw aluminum panel skin was left unpainted. It was only painted a dark blue with its code *"D-INJR"* applied in large white letters prior to being placed in the Berlin Aviation Museum. Scale model and photograph by *Günter Sengfelder.*

and a very complicated undercarriage retraction system. The *He 112* appeared to many to be a better flying machine than *Messerschmitt's Bf 109*. Although the *Bf 109* had better performance in climb and dive tests, people were still surprised to learn that in October 1935 the *Technisch Amt* selected the *Messerschmitt Bf 109* over *Heinkel's He 112*.

The winning *Bf 109* was proclaimed a "wonder fighter" by *Dr. Josef Goebbels' Ministry of Propaganda*, and the machine made its first public appearance in August at the 1936 11th Olympiad held in Berlin. At that time the Olympic Games still included flying competitions. Later, German propaganda was really able to taunt world governments, saying that their *Bf 109B* was indeed a superior world-class flying machine. This came to be because three so-called production *Bf 109Bs* powered by specially boosted *Daimler-Benz DB 600Ao* inverted *Vee* 12 engines—having maybe 1.5 times more horsepower than the typical *Bf 109* of its day, with 950 horsepower—dominated the 4th International Military Aircraft Competition, held at Zürich-Dübendorf, Switzerland, in July 1937. Overall, these three *Bf 109s* won the *Circuit of the Alps Race, the Alpenflug,* and the *Dive and Climb Race.* One of the three machines, the *Bf 109 V13,* was piloted by *Dipl.-*

Ing. Carl Francke, Chief of Test Flying for Fighters at the *RLM's Travemünde Erprobungsstelle. Francke,* in the Dive and Climb Competition, climbed to almost 10,000 feet [3,000 meters] and then dived the *Bf 109 V13* to 1,000 feet [300 meters] in just a little over two minutes. Had this performance been achieved by a military production fighter of its day, the world would certainly have been impressed and taken notice, because no other standard military fighter in any country could come even close to this climb and dive performance.

At the same 4th International Military Aircraft Competition, Germany also won the air speed circuit for multi-engine flying machines. The *Dornier Do 17M V1 (alias V8),* also with two especially prepared *DB 600Ao* inverted *Vee* 12 engines coupled to three-bladed *VDM* propellers for the occasion (same engine used in the *Bf 109 V13*) won with a level top air speed of 264 mph [425 km/h]...making it faster than France's *Dewoitine 510* fighter. But if the *Do 17M V1* was not Germany's standard twin engine military machine, the *Bf 109 V13* was not Germany's standard fighter type, either. In place of its standard *Daimler-Benz (DB)* inverted 60° *Vee* 12 of about 950 horsepower, the *Bf 109 V13* had, as was noted above, a specially modified *DB 601* en-

gine capable of producing 1,650 horsepower for short period bursts for high-speed air record attempts. A dead give-away was its M*esserschmitt V9* three-bladed propeller, rather than the standard two bladed, fixed pitch, *Schwarz* wooden propeller the initial *Bf 109B* carried. It also had a pointed propeller spinner which blended with the tightly fitted nose cowling. The *V13's* cockpit canopy was lower and more streamlined than the production versions of the *Bf 109B,* while its tail dimensions and wing length had all been reduced. It appeared that neither the press nor the public had been told about the Bf 1*09 V13's* substantial modifications. The *Bf 109 V13* was a planned deception by *Josef Goebbels* to simply awe and warn the governments of Europe that *National Socialism* was the most powerful government in the world with the military hardware to back it up. But it was all a lie.

Then, on 11 November 1937 Germany's *Dr.-Ing. Hermann Wurster* took away *Howard Hughes'* crown as the world's fastest air land-plane pilot. *Hughes,* an American multi-millionaire aircraft designer, test pilot, and owner of his own aircraft manufacturing company, had established a *FAI* Absolute World Air Speed Record of 352.391 mph [567.115 km/h] at Santa Anna, California, on 13 September 1935. When *Howard Hughes* set the new air land speed mark in his own *Hughes H-1 Racer (NR-258Y)* it was already clear that the air speed records were getting so high that in order to break them it would be necessary to design a new prototype using the very latest techniques and equip them with the most powerful aero motors available. It meant, too, that only very rich men such as *Howard Hughes, Renault,* and so on could still compete in this highly rarified venture without any guaran-

A direct nose-on view of the Me 209 V1 and featuring its Messerschmitt P8 three-bladed propeller. Test pilot Dr.-Ing. Wurster said that the estimated 2,300 horsepower engine ran very unevenly, it ran hot, and fumes from the overheated engine came into the cockpit, requiring the constant use of an oxygen mask. Scale model and photograph by *Günter Sengfelder.*

tees of ultimate commercial success. For example, Ed Browning, owner of the air record-breaking ex-USAAF North American *Republic P-51 Mustang* "*Red Baron*" spent an estimated $300,000 outfitting the "*Red Baron*" to challenge the Absolute World Air Speed Record in 1979. So the air speed record-breaking machine was far removed from military aircraft...unless a government, for reasons of prestige, set out to conquer the records. This is precisely what happen in Germany.

The De*utsches Reich* began pouring money into the construction of a *Messerschmitt AG*-designed air machine that would bring them the honors of having the world's fastest single-engine air land plane. Good results came almost immediately. *Dr.-Ing. Hermann Wurster, Bayerische Flugzeugwerke*'s (later renamed as *Messerschmitt AG*) chief test pilot, averaged 379.629 mph [610.960 km/h] in what German authorities told the *FAI* was a *Bf 113R*. In fact, this machine was derived pretty much from a standard *Messerschmitt Bf 109B* fighter aircraft powered by a *Daimler- Benz 600Ao* inverted 60° *Vee* 12 engine of about 950 nominal horsepower. It was coded *D-IPKY* and set an official 3-kilometer [1.86 mile] *FAI* Absolute World Air Speed Record for land planes. *FAI* regulations in the Summer of 1937 were a bit more relaxed than two years later when *Heinkel's Hans Dieterle* and *Messerschmitt's Fritz Wendel* each set *FAI* world speed records within 5 days of each other in August 1939. But in the Summer of 1937, a pilot challenging the existing world record had to make only four passes

(two in each direction) through the 1.86 mile course, and at an attitude not exceeding 245 feet. *Josef Goebbels* and other *NAZIs* insisted that the super smooth surface of the *Bf 113R,* which helped reduce wind resistance and, heretofore, had been used only on racing and record breaking air machines, was really only a standard production *Bf 109B* model of the time. Such silky smooth finishing was not and had not been used on production machines by any country. As one might imagine, few details and photographs were given out by German authorities at the time about their so-called *Bf 113R*. Today, of course, we know that *Dr.-Ing. Wurster* was piloting the *Messerschmitt Bf 109E V13* and that it was similar to the later *Bf 109Es*. The factory stated 950 horsepower of its engine was nominal power, that is, knowledge available to the whole world at that time, was that an aero-engine such as the 950 horsepower *Daimler-Benz* could be pushed to at least 1400/1500 horsepower. Indeed, by 1937 aero engine specialists were routinely able to almost double the nominal power for a 30 minute air record attempt.

In mid 1937 Ernst H*einkel* and *Willy Messerschmitt* had pretty much ceased to be friendly with one another. They never had been that close, anyway, but it grew chillier after *Messerschmitt's* surprising win of the *RLM's* design competition for a new mono wing fighter to replace the aging bi-wing *He 51* fighter. *Messerschmitt* won the competition with his *Bf 109* fighter prototype. Prior to the *RLM* selecting the *Bf 109, Ernst Heinkel* had started to build a dedicated air speed record machine with his own money based on his failed *He 112* prototype fighter. This new fighter prototype, a racing machine really, was initially known as the *Heinkel He 113* from the time it was on the drawing boards in 1937, but later received a different designation...changed by the superstitious *RLM* to the *He 100*. Nevertheless, this aircraft was a smooth, aerodynamically and beautifully styled machine designed by the gifted *Günter* twins: *Walter* and *Siegfried*. Unfortunately, *Walter* never lived to see their *He 100* fly. He died as a result of complications due to an automobile accident on 21 September 1937. He had lost one of his lungs as a soldier in WWI. Walter *Günter*

A direct tail-on view of the Me 209 V1. Its Daimler-Benz engine was cooled via surface radiators, which also incorporated evaporative cooling. When this machine flew a trail of vaporized water (steam) was seen in its wake...losing about two gallons of water per flight. In the fuselage was a water tank holding between 48 and 60 gallons, which allowed it to remain airborne for approximately 35 minutes because the water became overheated to steam and lost its cooling ability. Scale model and photograph by *Günter Sengfelder*.

thrilled in driving fast autos, and when he had the accident and damaged his remaining lung it wasn't able to keep him alive. Prior to designing the He *100 "racer,"* the *Günter* twins had given *Ernst Heinkel AG* the famous air speed record-breaking *He 70 "Blitz."* The *He 100 V1* made its first flight on 22 January 1938, and by June 1938 the *He 100 V2* had captured the *FAI's* World's Absolute Air Speed Record for 100 kilometers [62 miles] over a closed course, at 394 mph [634 km/h], even faster than *Messerschmitt's Bf 109 V13* had achieved on its short straight-line sprint. The *He 100* was actually a prototype fighter, unlike the *Bf 109 V13*, although many of its features would never be found on a front-line fighter. Surface radiators were used similar to those found on racing sea planes, such as the American *Curtiss*, the British *Supermarine*, and the Italian *Macchi*. While effective for short sprints, surface evaporation (radiators) could not absorb even the slightest damage to their wing surface. Were they to do so they would lose all their coolant. This was because heated water pumped out from the engine

and was circulated as steam under the wing's aluminum covering. Within the wing the steam condensed back to water and was reticulated back to the engine. Nevertheless, *Heinkel's* first three *He 100* prototypes (as many as eight may have been built) *V1, V2,* and *V3* were constructed with wing surface cooling. Then, three more prototypes were built, the *V4, V5,* and *V6,* however, their surface cooling was replaced by retractable belly radiators. It is commonly believed that H*einkel AG* built only six *He 100* racing prototypes, although there are some aviation historians who believe that as many as eight of these machines may have been constructed. In addition, about twelve pre-production versions were produced and given the designation of *He 100D.* They never entered service with the *Luftwaffe,* but *Dr. Goebbels* had them painted dark blue with black letter codes with the *halkenkreuz* on its wings and fuselage sides and *balkenkruez* on its rudder. The purpose of all this effort was to show the world that Germany already had several squadrons of these machines. Then *Goebbels* had their

former *He 113* designation reestablished, that is, returned to these propaganda machines. Of the six *He 113* prototypes constructed, one was destroyed in a flight test, one went to the *Deutsches Museum,* and the remaining six were sold to the USSR. Japan purchased three pre-production *He 113 D-Os,* too, while about twelve production machines known as *He 113D* were kept by *Ernst Heinkel* for defense of his Rostock aircraft manufacturing facility should they be attacked. If so, they would be piloted by *Ernst Heinkel AG* test pilots. It is believed that they saw no action as fighter interceptors.

While E*rnst Heinkel* was designing and building his racing *He 100* in 1937, there would be about a two-year lapse in record attempts...between November 1937 and August 1939. No new speed records had been established since *Dr.-Ing. Wurster* reached 379.629 mph [610.960 km/h] piloting the *Messerschmitt BF 109E V13 (Bf113R)* on 11 November 1937. However, two new *FAI* land air speed records were established within the month of August in 1939. *Hans Dieterle* was first in the *Heinkel 100 V8,* and then the second, only five days later, was set by *Fritz Wendel* in the *Messerschmitt Me 209 V1.* Both machines had been presented to the press at the time by *Josef Goebbels* as the *He 112U* and *Bf 109R* to suggest that they were direct derivatives of in-service fighter aircraft. The only authorized photographs given out at the time, too, did not allow any characteristic details to be identified. Even the documents *Messerschmitt AG* sent to the *FAI* do not say much.

As mentioned above, initially *Ernst Heinkel* constructed three *He 100* air speed record-breaking racer prototypes. The first one, the *He 100 V1,* made its maiden flight on 22 January 1938 with a factory standard 1,100 horsepower *Daimler-Benz DB 601A.* It was *Ernst Heinkel's* plan to go after the *FAI* Absolute Air Speed Record of 440.678 mph [709.202 km/h] held

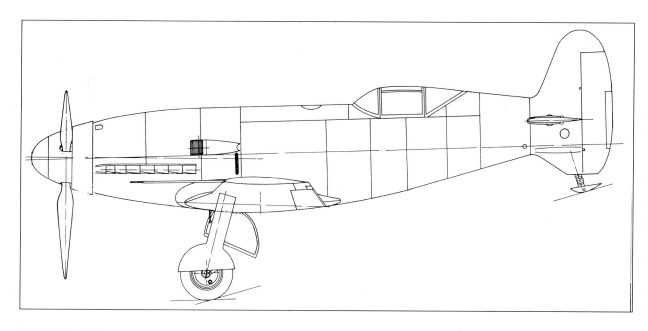

Pen and ink drawing of the Me 209 V1 and featuring its port side. Drawing by Günter Sengfelder.

by Italy's *Francesco Agello*. (*Agello* would later die in 1942 in an airplane accident.) The second machine, the *He 100 V2* coded *D-IVOS*, and also carrying a factory standard 1,100 horsepower D*B 601A*, was flight tested by *Ernst Udet* on 6 June 1938. *Udet* established a new 100 kilometer course record of 394 mph [634 km/h]. *Dr. Josef Goebbels* announced to the world's press that the machine *General Udet* was flying was the *He 112U*..."*U*' for *Udet*, it is imagined.

Ernst Udet's speed of 394 mph was only about 46 mph [74 km/h] slower than *Francesco Agello's FAI* world-setting land air speed record. Now *Ernst Heinkel* believed that he had the machine to break *Agello's* record. He selected his company's chief test pilot, *Gerhard Nitschke*, to be the man piloting the third *He 100* prototype. However, in this prototype coded *D-ISVR* had been installed a new *Daimler-Benz* highly modified, highly boosted *DB 601* in August 1938. In order to cut drag *Ernst Heinkel AG* engineers had reduced the wing-span of the *He 100 V3* to 24 feet 11.5 inches from 30 feet 10 inches and wing area to 118 square feet from 155 square feet. Then the new wing was attached to the *He 100 V3's* fuselage, along with a special low-drag cockpit canopy and the signature *Günter* twins glass-smooth surface finish. The *Daimler-Benz DB 601* had been reworked by increasing its revolutions-per-minute (rpm) to 3,000 from a factory setting of 2,300, injection of methyl-alcohol, special high-performance spark plugs, and so on, until a maximum output of between 1,700 to 1,800 horsepower was being obtained.

Preparations for the *FAI* Absolute Land Air Speed Record attempt were completed at Warneumünde on the Baltic Sea coast about June 1938. In September 1938, during a flight test of the *He 100 V3* by *Gerhard Nitschke*, an undercarriage leg stuck in the retracted position, and *Nitschke* was forced to bale out, injuring himself in the process when he struck part of the *He*

100 V3's* tail. *Don Berliner*, author of the 1983 book *Victory Over The Wind*, relates a conversation he had with *Hans Dieterle* regarding the *Heinkel He 100 V3*:

In order to reduce unnecessary aerodynamic drag, all irregularities on the body and wings were smoothed and the whole airplane was polished. Furthermore, the engine power of 1,000 horsepower was increased to 1,800 by increasing the manifold pressure in connection with higher revolutions per minute. The high thermic stresses of such a turned motor could be mastered only with a special fuel. This fuel had the capacity to absorb heat from the engine for cooling and to function at high compression ratios without preigniting. Special heat-resistant spark plugs were necessary; however, they fouled at low engine performance.

It is obvious that these extremely strained engines had a rather short life. The engine builder estimated a 30-minute running life.

As a last measure, this plane was fitted with a special propeller which was very effective at high speeds; it showed rather low acceleration at takeoff, however.

Due to the many modifications, the plane was very sensitive, and so difficult to fly that it had to be handled like a raw egg. I had been given the order to undertake the necessary test flights. At that time I was only a young company pilot; therefore, the chief pilot for Ernst Heinkel AG was supposed to do the last test flight and the actual record flight. Unfortunately, this never happened. During the last test flight, in September 1938, the landing gear jammed, and when the

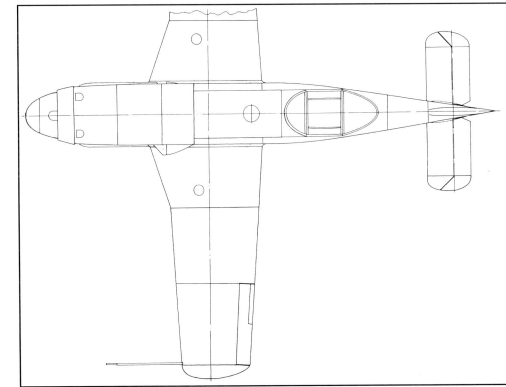

Pen and ink drawing of the Me 209 V1 and featuring its overall planview as seen from above. Drawing by *Günter Sengfelder*.

engine suddenly seized, the pilot was forced to leave the plane by parachute. The real reasons for that disaster were never found out.

The loss of his beloved He 100 V3 airplane came as a shock to Dr. Heinkel, but he did not give up his plans, and had another *He 100* prepared as a new record-breaker...the He 100 V8. He now ordered that I should be the *pilot*.

Ernst Heinkel had three additional prototypes *V4* through *V7* under construction when the *V3* was lost...all powered by a factory standard *DB 601A*. With the loss of the *He 100 V3*, *Heinkel* picked the eighth prototype, their *He 100 V8*, to be his next dedicated racing machine. *Heinkel AG* test pilot *Gerhard Nitshke* was still recovering from injures sustained in his bail out of the *He 100 V2*. It was at this time that *Hans Dieterle* was selected by *Ernst Heinkel* to be the pilot of *He 100 V8* coded *D- ISUR*. As the *V8* was being made ready it was fitted, too, at first with a factory standard 1,100 horsepower *DB 601A* engine so that test pilot *Dieterle* could gain experience on this machine. Later, an estimated 1,800 horsepower *Daimler-Benz* engine known as the *DB 601R* was installed for the attempt on the Absolute World Air Speed Record.

The *He 100 V8* would have even less wingspan than the three previous *He 100*s...24 feet 9 inches [7.6 meters] from 30 feet 9 inches [9.4 meters]. The following is what *Heinkel AG* company test pilot *Hans Dieterle* told *Don Berliner* regarding the *He 100 V8*:

By the end of February 1939, the V8 was finished. The record trials were now done at the Heinkel subsidiary at Oranienburg, near Berlin...because there was a longer runway and...less disturbance for our team, consisting of about 25 people. I looked around for an appropriate racing line and found one that went along a railway track. With a standard He 100D, which I had been given for that purpose, I made as many trial runs as possible.

After each run, I reduced engine power somewhat, and at about 400 meters [1,300 feet] altitude I directed myself to the turning point, which was at a distance of 20 to 25 kilometers [12 to 16 miles]. From the turning point I turned at full power to the race course and reduced my altitude to below 75 meters [245 feet]. It was very important that I know the landscape, offhand, since the plane allowed only limited view, due to the cockpit modifications.

The Heinkel He 100 V8 was first flown with a standard motor in order to define the last-minute modifications. To minimize the risk for the plane, only necessary flights were made. After the plane had received its special engine, it started for its first attack on the existing record; but it had to be stopped short at the approach to the race course because the engine started to vibrate and did not develop its full power. We found out later that the carburetor could not...provide the quantity of fuel which this engine needed. This motor was very "thirsty," and needed up to 300 gallons [1,135 liters] per hour.

After the existing fuel pump was replaced by a higher capacity one, I started my second try, which was unsuccessful, also. I had already passed the racing distance twice [apparently, *Dieterle* means he completed two passes over the course] when I was forced to land due to high oil temperature that was too high and too low oil pressure. This He 100 had none of the conventional oil coolers because they could have created aerodynamic disturbance. The hot oil ran through a heat exchanger, located in the fuselage behind the pilot's seat. It was cooled by methyl-alcohol, which has a very low evaporation temperature. When the oil reached 65°C [150°F], the methyl-alcohol evaporated and thus cooled off the oil by dissipating heat. The alcohol vapors were cooled in the wings and condensed back to liquid alcohol, which was then pumped back by little pumps to the heat exchanger...this cooling system could not handle the extreme heat that developed when the engine ran at full power.

The two trials and the different, standard runs already accounted for a running time of the engine of about half an hour. Therefore, there was a high risk that the engine might fail very soon. The good news from these trials was that our measurements taken showed the *He 100 V8* was fast enough to break the (*FAI*) air speed record of the Italian Agello.

Direct starboard side view of the Me 209 V1. Dr.-Ing. Wurster said that visibility from the cockpit was severely limited and blamed the fact that the cockpit was placed well aft on the fuselage. Scale model and photograph by *Günter Sengfelder*.

On March 30, 1939, the weather was okay, and I decided to make another take-off. However, my "taking off" was not as easy as the words sound. For every takeoff, my "ballerina" needed a great deal of preparation. She was hauled to the runway; there she was faced into the wind and warmed up using normal spark plugs. When the running temperature was reached, the engine was shut off. Specialists of the engine builder exchanged, as quickly as possible, the standard plugs with so-called racing plugs. This had to be done extremely fast in order to prevent the motor from cooling off too much.

In the meantime, I had taken my cockpit seat, buckled myself in, and started the engine again. Because of the sensitive spark plugs, the motor could run only at high speed. Since the motor did not run smoothly, I had no way to control it by feel. This was done by the engineers of the engine-builder, who checked the exhaust flames of the twelve cylinders and only let the plane take off when this analysis was to their satisfaction.

The wheel chocks were taken away, and the bird started rolling. My big problem was to get up speed, since I had only moderate acceleration with the special propeller. At the end of the runway, a large colored flag was posted to serve for direction.

Time after time, I directed my plane to the "racing track," with the firm intention to risk more than usual. Within thirteen minutes between take-off and landing, I flew the racing distance four times, each time pushing the throttle to maximum and not being as critical with the temperature control as before.

Heinkel AG's He 100 V8 was equipped with a *DB 601E* probably producing a nominal 1,175 horsepower, like the *Messerschmitt Bf 109 V13*, and one suspects that the effective power would have been closer to 2,000 horsepower. But the increase in power between the 379.629 mph [610.960 km/h] of *Hermann Wurster's Bf 109 V13* and the 463.921 mph [746.604 km/h] of *Dieterle's He 100 V8*, or the 469.225 mph [755.138 km/h] of *Fritz Wendel's Me 209 V1*...about 500 to 600 horsepower or some 30%...is not sufficient to explain the enormous increase in speed achieved. It would have been necessary to have 85% more power between the *Bf 109 V13* and the *Me 209 V1*. In addition, it was necessary to have a very refined airframe with good high lift devices to increase the wind loading to 175-180 kilograms/meters squared, and the aircraft's wing needed to be reduced in size as much as possible; 14.5 meters squared for the H*einkel* and 13.2 for the *Messerschmitt*, the smaller of the two. Their take-off weights were respectively 5,732 pounds [2,600 kilograms] for the *Heinkel* and 5,071 pounds [2,300 kilograms] for the *Messerschmitt Me 209V1*. After its Absolute World Air Speed Record-breaking duties were over the *He 100 V8* was sent to the *Deutsches* Museum-Munich. The Museum was destroyed during a bombing raid in July 1944 by the U.S. 8th Air Force, and along with it the world's first turbojet powered aircraft, the *Heinkel He 176*. It is not known to this author what became of the air speed record-setting *Bf 109 V13*.

Specifications: *He 100 V8*
Wing span - 24 feet 9 inches [7.6 meters]
Length, overall - 26 feet 8 inches [8.2 meters]
Height, overall - 8 feet 2 inches [2.5 meters]
Weight, take off - about 5,600 pounds [2,537 kilograms]
Engine - *Daimler-Benz DB 601R* producing an estimated 1,800 horsepower
Engine life - about 30 minutes

General Ernst Udet, director of the *RLM's Technisch Amt*, publically accepted *Messerschmitt's* offer and gave him a contract—a secret kept from H*einkel* for a while, and others—for the construction of four experimental high-speed machines through which to make an attack on *Ernst Heinkel's FAI* Absolute World Air Speed Record of 469.224 mph [755.138 km/h]. The first *Messerschmitt AG* machine (*Project 1059*) was given the designation of *Me 209* by the *RLM* and became officially known as the *Me 209 V1*. It was to be powered by a specially modified but standard *DB 601A* engine of about a nominal 1,100 horsepower. Publicly, Jo*sef Goebbels* was calling this machine the *Bf 109R* to convince the world governments that it really was merely one of their front-line fighters.

Nose starboard side view of the Me 209 V1. Test pilot Dr.-Ing. Wurster said that the V1's take off run was excessive, and called its rotation "filled with vicious characteristics." Scale model and photograph by *Günter Sengfelder*.

The *RLM's* initial order called for three prototypes to be built, and they each received civil registrations: D-INJR, D-IWAH, and D-IVFP. *Messerschmitt AG werk nummern* assigned were *1185, 1186,* and *1187,* respectively. Since *Udet* had followed his advisors' advice and accepted the *Bf 109* as Germany's front line fighter, further work was in order. If they had to carry out the "bluff" that Germany now had the fastest fighter in the world, it would have to carry the world's air land speed record, too. *Udet,* who was a friend of *Heinkel,* explained to him later:

Good Lord, *Ernst,* it simply won't do for the rest of the world for a fighter like the *He 100,* which has not been selected for mass production, to hold the record and the *Bf 109,* which everyone knows is our standard fighter, not to. Therefore, that's all there is to it, and I don't like your idea of another record attempt (to beat the *Me 209 V-1).*

The plan was that the M*e 209* would follow on the success of the *Bf 109E V13 (Bf 113R)* when it established a world air speed record of 380 mph [611 km/h] in 11 November 1937. But the *Me 209* was designed specifically as a speed record-breaking machine to surpass the record of 463.9 mph [746.6 km/h] set by the *Heinkel He 100 V8.* While the *He 100 V8* was originally an experimental fighter prototype and appearing similar to the failed *He 112,* the *Me 209* was solely a high-speed research aircraft, and it bore no resemblance to the *Bf 109*...Germany's new front-line fighter.

Ernst Udet, after all, was no stranger to high speed machines, daring aerobatics, and setting air speed records, but it had to have been very difficult for *Udet,* a long time friend of *Ernst Heinkel,* to tell him that the *NAZI Partei,* especially *Goebbels,* wanted the next world air record to be held by a *Bf 109* and that the *RLM* was giving money to *Willy Messerschmitt* to finance the construction of several machines whose only purpose was to break the *Heinkel He 100 V8's FAI* Absolute World Air Speed Record. It had to be doubly hard, too, because *Udet* was not a member of the *NAZI Partei* and often referred to them as "swine." On the other hand, the *NAZIs* doubted *Udet's* allegiance and believed that he was more sympatric to the United States of America than to the *Third Reich. Udet* had visited America many times appearing in Hollywood movies, performing stunts, and doing aerobatics throughout the country. He was impressed by America's industrial might and vast natural resources. When he was appointed head of the *Technisch Amt* of the *RLM,* he cautioned his colleagues that no country in the world would ever win a prolonged war with America due to their high-technology, skilled work force, mass production, and staggering wealth of natural resources. But many merely laughed, saying that the only thing America was good at was making nice double-edged razor blades. Getting back to our story, *Udet* himself had brought the world's air speed record to Germany for the first time, although unofficial, by flying *Ernst Heinkel's He 100 V2* at an air speed of 394.2 mph [634.4 km/h] and bettering the unofficial air speed record then held by the Italian *Niclot* by more than 50 miles per hour [80.5 km/h]. *Heinkel AG* would go on to better *Ernst Udet's* record-breaking performance by making it official. On 30 March 1939, 24 year old H*ans Dieterle* took the rebuilt *He 100 V8,* with its upwards of 1,800 to 2,000 horsepower *DB 601* engine, up in the late afternoon, about 5:30 p.m. *Dieterle* flew the *He 100 V8* at an average speed of 463.921 mph [746.588 km/h], and Germany now held the *FAI's* Absolute World Air Speed Record for the first time in its history. It could have been faster, because *Hans Dieterle* flew the *100 V8* at a very low altitude of only 245 feet where the air was thick and robbing him of a higher speed. For this achievement *Ernst Heinkel* was awarded the *NAZI National Prize for Art and Science.* At the *Nuremburg Partei Tag* on 1 September

A good view of the Me 209 V1's general planform as seen from above and behind. Scale model and photograph by *Reinhard Roeser.*

1939, *Heinkel*, *Todt*, *Porsche*, and *Messerschmitt* each received the *National Prize*. Even *Heinkel's* selection for the *National Prize* was strongly opposed by *Martin Bormen*, however, *Hitler* himself over-ruled, stating that this rejection simply wouldn't be in the *NAZI Partei's* best interest.

Eventually, four *Me 209* prototypes were constructed. However, the first three machines had wing spans of 25.6 feet [7.8 meters] and fuselage overall lengths of 23.7 feet [7.24 meters]. They were all nicknamed the "*Flying Eber*," or flying boar (pig). Power was provided by a single standard issue *DB 601A* liquid-cooled inverted 60° *Vee* 12 engine. In the *Me 209 V1*, fuel and cooling water tanks were located at the machine's center of gravity in the fuselage aft the engine. The pilot's cockpit was positioned well aft the center of gravity, and barely forward its vertical/ventral stabilizer fin. This fin was extended in the ventral position, too, to help counterbalance the huge propeller torque. The amount of cooling water was reported to be between 48 and 60 gallons. A vapor cooling system was adopted for the *Me 209 V1*, in which the engine's cooling water when heated to steam was condensed back to liquid water in a short rectangular radiator located in the wing's center section, at its trailing edge. Thus, the water could be used again, while part of the water was discarded through vents in the upper surface of the wing. The consumption ratio of water lost to evaporation was between 1 and 1.5 gallons [4 and 5 liters] per minute...about 2 gallons [9 liters] maximum. A small ring-shaped oil cooler/radiator was installed aft the propeller hub/spinner.

Me 209 V1

The first *Me 209* prototype, the *209 V1*, (*Werk Nummer 1185* and coded *D-INJR*) known around *Messerschmitt AG* as project *P-1059*, began its life late in 1937 and was completed in June 1938. It flew for the first time

The *Me 209 V1* as seen from its nose starboard side. Scale model and photograph by *Günter Sengfelder*.

on 1 August 1938, but only for seven minutes. It was all aluminum, and *Messerschmitt AG* engineers kept its natural aluminum color thoroughout all of its test flights...its various aluminum panels appearing light or dark. It was only painted a deep dark blue after it was taken to the Berlin Air Museum and put on public display with its code D-*INJR* painted in large white letters. In fact, a series of publicity photos showing *Fritz Wendel* in the cockpit with *Willy Messerschmitt* standing by the machine's port side and shaking his hand were all photographed at the Berlin Air Museum. From the very beginning a series of troubles with the *Me 209 V1's* cooling system and undercarriage appeared. And what did *Dr.-Ing. Hermann Wurster* think of his first flight, which lasted seven minutes? The following are his own comments, found postwar in captured documents from *Messerschmitt AG's* achieves. Pilot *Hermann Wurster* reported:

01. The engine runs unevenly;
02. The high temperature reached by the coolant fluid results in unsatisfactory cooling;
03. Cockpit ventilation is inadequate, and engine gases penetrate the cockpit, necessitating the constant use of an oxygen mask;
04. The undercarriage cannot be extended at speeds in excess of 250 km/h [155 mph];
05. The main wheels tend to drop out of their wheel wells during high speed maneuvers;
06. Fuel filler cap covers tend to lift off at high speed;
07. Undercarriage hydraulic oil escapes from its reservoir and sprays the windscreen;
08. The take-off run is excessive, and the take-off characteristics vicious;
09. Visibility from the cockpit is severely limited;
10. Marked instability manifests itself during the climb;
11. The rudder is inadequate to control the plane in a bank;
12. When banking at full throttle, the plane rolls over on its back;
13. Stick forces are excessive and tiring;
14. At speeds in the vicinity of 160 to 170 km/h [100 to 105 mph] the controls soften up;

15. Landing characteristics are extremely dangerous, except under windless conditions;

16. On touch down, the plane swerves violently;

17. It is impossible to employ the brakes during the landing run, as immediately when they are applied, the aircraft swerves from the runway.

If any aircraft prototype had experienced just a few of the above seventeen criticisms, it is likely that the machine would have been abandoned. But the *NAZI Partei* didn't care. Their attitude was to make it fly fast and fly fast enough to beat the *Heinkel 100 V8*. So testing continued, even though the slightest error on the part of the pilot, as *Wurster* remarked, could result in his death. Throughout August 1938, *Daimler-Benz* engineers were able to substantially improve the

The Me 209 V1 shown in a banking turn. Dr. Wurster said in his written report that when he put the machine into a banking turn at full throttle, the plane would roll over on its back. In addition, the main wheels tended to drop out of their wheel wells during high-speed maneuvers. Scale model and photograph by *Günter Sengfelder*.

basic nominal 1,600 horsepower output of their *DB 601 ARJ* engine to a reported 2,300 horsepower. However, it was able to do this for only short bursts...but it could only be operated at its full horsepower for a short time, about 30 minutes, before it self destructed due to overheating of its lubricating oil and cooling water. During this short time of operation at its stated 2,300 horsepower, the *DB 601 ARJ* consumed 2 gallons [9 liters] of cooling water. With its approximately 50 gallons [450 liters] of cooling water on board the *Me 209 V1* could remain in the air for 35 minutes of normal operating ranges. So far so good, for an air speed record breaker. However, *Messerschmitt AG* suddenly had a new problem. *Willy Messerschmitt* had heard about *Ernst Heinkel's* achievement in capturing the

FAI Absolute World Air Speed Record for Germany...their first...from the famous Italian air speedster *Francesco Agello*. It had been four years since *Agello* had established the record at 440.678 mph [709.202 km/h], and this was in a *Macchi-Castoldi* seaplane. Now, eleven years of domination by seaplanes had been stopped by *Heinkel's He 100 V8* air land plane.

Messerschmitt's problem now was which of the three remaining *Me 209* air frames should he use for his highly modified *DB 601 ANJ*. Since the *Me 209 V2* had been completely destroyed in a flight test and *209 V3* and *209 V4* were still unfinished, *Messerschmitt* decided that he wouldn't wait for the completion of *V3* or *V4*; he'd place the new 2,300 horsepower *Daimler-Benz* in the *Me 209 V1,* instead, just to see how fast the machine would really fly. So, on 26 April 1939 test pilot *Fritz Wendel* flew the re-engined *209 V1* with its 2,300 horsepower *DB 601 ANJ* inverted *Vee* 12 engine. Everyone was stunned when *Wendel* flew the machine to a new *FAI* Absolute World Air Speed Record of 469.224 mph [755.138 km/h]. It was barely 6.0 mph [1.0 km/h] faster than *Heinkel's He 100 V8* record mark. Although the *FAI* required that an established record had to be surpassed by at least 01.0%, the *FAI* accepted the *Me 209 V1's* 6.0 mph over the *He 100 V8's* as good enough and gave the new record to *Messerschmitt AG. Josef Goebbels,* head of the German Propaganda Ministry, was elated, and then decreed that no further attempt by anyone in Germany would be allowed. *Ernst Heinkel* had planned to immediately recapture the world air speed record for himself, but *Josef Goebbels'* decree that no new air-speed record attempts would be tolerated put an end to his plans. *Ernst Heinkel* had lost out again...to the *NAZI Partei*. He had first lost the competition for Germany's new fighter, and now he'd been shut out of making any more attempts on the absolute world air speed record by only 6.0 mph! *Heinkel* could have very easily bettered it. It is widely believed that the *Me 209*

V1's DB 601 ANJ had some 500 to 600 more horsepower than did the *DB 601* used in the *He 100 V8*...maybe more. In addition, *Ernst Heinkel* wanted to fly the *He 100 V8* again, but this time at a higher elevation like *Fritz Wendel* did. He had flown the *Me 209 V1* at 1,323 feet [400 meters] higher than the *He 100 V8* where the air was thinner and more acceptable to a higher speed. *Heinkel's* engineers estimated that their *He 100 V8* could reach at least 478 mph [769 km/h] if he flew it at the same altitude the *Messerschmitt Me 209 V1* had been flown. But *Ernst Heinkel* was immediately officially barred from any further attempts by the *NAZI Partei* once the *Me 209 V1* had captured the record. Thus, the *FAI's* Absolute World Air Speed Record was destined to remain with *Messerschmitt AG*...which it did for over thirty years...until 14 August 1969, when the American *Darryl Greenamyer*, a *Lockheed* test pilot, flew his highly modified ex-WWII, U.S. Navy Grumman F8F-2 "*Bearcat*" to 482.462 mph [776.426 km/h]...13.238 mph [21.304 km/h] faster than *Fritz Wendel*.

Messerschmitt's Absolute World Air Record-setting *Me 209 V1* was retired to the Berlin Air Museum. Later, the *Heinkel He 178*, the world's first turbojet powered aircraft, became part of the Museum's collection, too, but it was destroyed in the same 1943 Royal Air Force (RAF) bombing raid that badly damaged the *Me 209 V1*. The remains of the *Me 209 V1*, along with several rare aircraft and rare aero engines, were known to have been pulled out of the burning museum and were reported to have been transported to Poland for safe-keeping. All this had been pretty much forgotten, and the *Me 209 V1* was considered lost, too, until in 1967, *Norman Wiltshire*, an Australian member of *Air Britain*, the International Association of Aviation Historians, discovered the remains of the *Me 209 V1* while exploring the Muzeum Lotnictwa Polskiego (Polish Air Museum), in Kracow, Poland. What was left of the *Me 209 V1* was only its fuselage aft the fire wall, but no engine and no wings. So, after decades of being considered no longer in existence, at least part of the famous air speed record-breaking aircraft had been found. Germany has offered the Poles a substantial sum of *Deutches Marks* from time to time for its remains, but as of the year 2000 the Poles have ignored Germany's continuous plea to please return the air record-setting machine to Berlin.

Specifications: *Me 209V1*
Wing span - 25 feet 6 inches [7.8 meters]
Wing area - 114.095 square feet [10.6 square meters]
Wing loading- 48.746 pounds per square inch
Length, overall - 23 feet 8 inches [7.3 meters]
Weight, loaded - 5,545 pounds [2,512 kilograms]
Speed, maximum - 469.224 mph [755.138 km/h]
Speed, cruising - unknown
Speed, landing - not available
Climb, maximum rate - unknown
Service ceiling - unknown
Flight duration - about 35 minutes
Engine: *DB 601 ARJ* producing an estimated 2,300 horsepower

Me 209 V2

The second *Me 209* prototype, the *209 V2* (*Werk Nummer 1186* and coded *D-IWAH*), made its first flight on 8 February 1939 piloted by *Dr.-Ing. Wurster*. Afterward *Hermann Wurster* left the flight testing program to concentrate on completely different engineering tasks within *Messerschmitt AG*...development of the air-to-ground missile known as the *Enzian*. When *Hermann Wurster* gave up test pilot duties to concentrate on guided missile development, *Fritz Wendel* became *Messerschmitt AG's* chief test pilot and the one to beat *Heinkel AG's FAI* Absolute World Air Speed Record. Later, on 4 August 1938, during a flight test by *Fritz Wendel*, the *Me 209 V2's* propeller reduction gear froze immediately after takeoff. *Wendel* crash landed the *V2*. He was somehow able to avoid serious injuries in the crash, but the *V2* would never fly again.

The Me 209 V1 appearing in flight and featuring its port side. The cockpit canopy's low wind resistance style later appeared on the Messerschmitt Bf 109 G-10. Dr. Wurster complained that undercarriage hydraulic oil escaped from its reservoir and it was sprayed all over the cockpit windscreen. Scale model and photograph by *Günter Sengfelder*.

Me 209 V3

The third Me 209 prototype, the 209 V3 (Werk Nummer 1187 coded D-IVFP) had been the machine of choice for Messerschmitt AG's attempt on the FAI's Absolute World Air Speed record, but it had not been completed until late May 1939...even after the Me 209 V4. The Me 209 V3 was the last of the three prototype racing machines to be completed with all funds provided by the RLM for the sole purpose of breaking the World Absolute Air Speed Record held by Heinkel AG, however, when it was completed it was already obsolete. It was used for experimental purposes, for example, testing with a larger wing with automatic leading-edge slots, and a new ventral radiator which had been installed in place of its surface evaporation cooling system.

Me 209 V4

The fourth Me 209 prototype, the 209 V4 (Werk Nummer 1188 and first coded D-IRND, then later in 1940 given a military code of CE+BW) is thought to have been built at Messerschmitt's own expense. It is unclear, however, if the V4 was completed as a prototype fighter, since the 209 V1 had already set a new Absolute World Air Speed Record. The V4 was first flown on 12 May 1939, and apparently the few design changes made in this machine did little to improve the overall flying characteristics of the Me 209, because Dr.-Ing. Wurster continued calling this type "one of those little monsters." This machine's fuselage was virtually the same as the other three high-speed 209's, with the exception that it was fitted with 2xMG 17 7.9 mm cannon, one engine mounted MG FF/M 20 mm cannon firing through the propeller hub, and 2xMK 108 30 mm cannon in the wing. All this heavy offensive cannon was installed with the hope that the V4 might replace the aging Bf 109. To further strengthen its role as a fighter, the V4's vertical and ventral tail was enlarged, the main undercarriage oleo struts shortened, and a new wing span measuring 30 feet

5.5 inches in length was constructed. Total wing area now was 119.15 square feet, and wing loading was 38 pounds per square inch. The single-spar stressed aluminum surface skin covered structure was fitted with automatic leading-edge slots and, probably, what appears to be slotted trailing-edge flaps, as well.

The Me 209 V4 was powered by a factory standard 1,100 rated horsepower DB 601A water cooled, inverted Vee 12 cylinder engine. Initially, Messerschmitt AG engineers kept the surface evaporation cooling system as used on the previous high-speed prototypes, but after repeated problems and troubles, it was replaced after its 8th flight test with a more conventional system comprised of low-drag radiators beneath its inboard wing panels. Even the results of this system were disappointing, as was its performance. Later in its flight test program, the wing was lengthened once, then again to an overall span of 32 feet 11.5 inches, and its automatic wing slots replaced by new leading edges. The DB 601A engine was replaced with a DB 601N of 1,200 take-off horsepower, however, with a loaded weight of 6,173 pounds, the 209 V4 was underpowered, and water and oil overheating continued to be persistent problems. A large ventral radiator replaced the two smaller low-drag radiators...half buried radiators like the ones used on the Bf 109 were installed under the machine's wing beneath the fuselage at the trailing edge. However, when the 209 V4 was flight tested this way, its performance dropped below that of the existing Bf 109Es coming off Messerschmitt AG production lines, and its handling characteristics remained vicious and difficult, even for the most experienced pilot. All these defects and short-comings were the reason for the abandonment of the Me 209 V4 as a high-speed fighter prototype.

The Heinkel AG bi-wing He 51. It was put into Luftwaffe service in 1933 with a maximum speed of 200 mph and a service ceiling of 25,000+ feet. It was usually armed with 2xMG 17 cannons. After the Bf 109 replaced it about 1938, the old bi-wing still served, although as a trainer. Approximately 700 He 51 machines were manufactured between 1933 and 1938.

Specifications: *Me 209V4*

Wing span - 32 feet 11.5 inches [10.04 meters]
Wing area - 119.15 square feet
Wing loading - 38 pounds per square inch
Length, overall - 23 feet 9 inches [7.24 meters]
Height - not available
Weight, loaded - 6,174 pounds [2,800 kilograms]
Speed, maximum at 19,680 feet [6,000 meters] - 373 mph [600 km/h]
Speed, cruising at 16,400 feet [5,000 meters] - 311 mph [500 km/h]
Speed, landing - not available
Climb, maximum rate - 3,690 feet/minute [1,125 meters/minute]
Service ceiling - 36,080 feet [11,000 meters]
Flight duration - unknown
Engine - *Daimler-Benz DB 601A* producing a nominal horsepower of about 1,100 and later re-engined with a D*B 601N* providing about 1,200 horsepower

Other *Me 209* Deviations

There was also a machine known as the *Me 209 V5*. It was offered to the *RLM* by *Messerschmitt AG* in competition with the *Focke-Wulf Ta 152*. The *Me 209 V5* is sometimes known, too, as the *Bf 209 II*, or the *Me 209A*. On 23 April 1943 the *RLM* had issued a request for a high-altitude fighter. The *Me 209 V5* was very different from the earlier four *Me 209* world air speed record prototypes. Instead, this version used a lot of parts and pieces from the *Bf 109G*, including its rear fuselage, which had been extended to a longer length, longer wing span (35 feet 11 inches [10.95 meters]), tail wheel strut, a straight trailing edge on the rudder, and so on, appearing very similar to the *Bf*

Aces of World War One. Left to right: Ernst Udet, Bruno Loezer, and Baron Manfred von Richthofen. Udet and Loezer survived the conflict, and Udet went on to become the 4th highest scoring ace in the world. Upon seeing the *Bf 109* prototype for the first time, *Udet* remarked to *Willy Messerschmitt* that the machine would never do as a fighter because of the enclosed cockpit. *Udet* was still thinking WWI and bi-planes...much the same as did Hermann Gö*ring*...*Udet's* boss.

109 G-10. It was coded *SP+LJ* and was first flight tested on 3 November 1943 by *Fritz Wendel* with its *DB 603A* and spinning an 11 foot 1.5 inch three-bladed *Messerschmitt P8* propeller. A second prototype, the *Me 209 V6*, was completed, and it made its maiden flight on 22 December 1943. A third prototype, the *Me 209 V7*, underwent an engine change after its first test flight with the installation of a D*B 603G*, including a taller vertical stabilizer. Its first test flight with the *DB 603G* was on 12 November 1943. This machine was fitted with a *Jumo 213E* inverted *Vee* 12-cylinder liquid-cooled engine and was equipped with a annular radiator. It drove a 10 foot 6 inch *Junkers* three-bladed *VS 19* propeller. Both the *V5* and *V6* prototypes had about equal performance from their powerful *Daimler-Benz* engines. Maximum speed of the *Me 209 V7*—later redesignated by the *RLM* as the *Me 209A-2*—

achieved was between 410 and 417 mph. Another M*e 209* prototype was constructed and was given the *RLM* designation of *Me 209H V1*. This machine was completed about June 1944 and test flown with a *DB 603G* engine up through mid January 1945 when, about this time, all further work and testing was abandoned on the remaining *Messerschmitt AG Me 209* fighter prototypes.

Founder, chief executive officer, and president of Heinkel AG...Ernst Heinkel. He blamed the loss of the RLM's fighter competitions to his development chief Dr.-Ing. Heinrich Hertel. *Heinkel* wrote, post war, that it was *Dr. Hertel*, who when building the *He 112* brought along his tendency for endless changes, experimentations, and novelties, and in doing so was the final reason that the *He 112* was completed long after the *Bf 109*, thus losing the competition for Germany's next generation fighter.

Willy Messerschmitt and Hubert Bauer admiring several scale models of aircraft currently in serial production. Shown is a Bf 108 and two *Bf 109s*.

A poor quality photo of the Soviet Polikarpov I-16 "Rata," or Rat, as seen from its port side. This machine was a veteran of the Spanish Civil War, where it proved to be superior to the *He 51* biplane...at least up until the time the *Bf 109* was introduced in the civil conflict in 1937.

Left to right, the old and the new: the old Heinkel He 51 biplane and the new Bf 109 mono plane fighter prototype coded D-IABI of the Bayerische Flugzeug Werke (BFW). Scale models and photograph by *Günter Sengfelder*.

Port side of the Messerschmitt Bf 109 prototype fighter. This machine, during testing, was found to be faster, lighter, a more simple design, and cheaper to build than any of its other three competitors. Scale model and photograph by *Günter Sengfelder*.

The rear port side of the Messerschmitt Bf 109 prototype fighter. When the RLM's test pilots at Rechlin tested the new machine from Messerschmitt they discovered that it had a weak undercarriage prone to causing ground loops. In addition, test pilots did not like the *Bf 109's* side-opening cockpit canopy. Scale model and photograph by *Günter Sengfelder*.

Nose starboard side of the Messerschmitt Bf 109 prototype fighter. On 15 April 1936, Dr.-Ing Hermann Wurster, Messerschmitt AG's chief test pilot, gave a demonstration of the *Bf 109 V2's* abilities in competition with *Heinkel AG's* chief test pilot, *Gerhard Nitschke*, piloting the *He 112 V1*. *Wurster* began by taking the machine up to 22,966 ft [7,000 meters] altitude and then putting it into a dive, pulling up just above the ground and subjecting himself and the *V2* machine to 7.8 g's. Then he put the machine through a spin demonstration at 7,874 ft [2,400 meters] altitude, making 21 rotations to the right and 17 to the left. *Gerhard Nitschke* was next in the *He 112 V1*. Reaching 7,874 ft [2,400 meters], he started putting the *V1* into left spins but went into a flat stall and then nosed over into a flat spin. *Nitschke* said that he tried every trick in the book to recover the machine but couldn't. He bailed out at about 1,640 ft [500 meters] and watched the *He 112 V1* crash down in or near a levee in full sight of the crowd. Afterward, the *Bf 109 V2* prototype was declared the winner. Scale model and photograph by *Günter Sengfelder*.

Nose port side view of the Bf 109 V2. Scale model and photograph by *Günter Seng-felder.*

The nose of the Bf 109 prototype fighter with its *Jumo 210* engine and featuring its two bladed, fixed pitch, *Schwarz* wooden propeller. Scale model and photograph by *Günter Sengfelder*.

The loser in the RLM's mono wing fighter competition...the Heinkel He 112V1. It was destroyed on 15 April 1936 when it entered into a flat spin and its pilot *Gerhard Nitschke* bailed out. The *V1* is shown here with its two-bladed *HKW* (*Heidenheimer KupferWerke*) propeller.

RLM's Rechlin test pilots found the He 112 to have a rugged construction and were pleased with its flight handling characteristics. This machine fully met all the *RLM's* requirements handed down in their request for proposals. But the *He 112* was more expensive in terms of labor costs to manufacture than *Messerschmitt's Bf 109*...about two times as long to manufacture. *Heinkel* kept on trying to change on this with his *He 112*, but the impatient *RLM* selected the *Bf 109* while the *He 112* lagged behind undergoing modification after modification to make it more competitive.

The He 112 V10, seen here with its DB 601 and three-bladed VDM propeller. With these and a few other additions, the He 112 V10 was now equal with the *Bf 109*...in several ways better...however, the *RLM* had made its selection months prior, and the *V10* by *Heinkel* didn't matter anymore. *Ernst Heinkel* could, if he wished, seek to sell his *He 112* to foreign buyers, but for various reasons it was a hard sell and he didn't move many of his machines.

The He 112 V10 coded D-IGSI seen from the ground looks much like the British Spitfire fighter of WWII. It would have been fascinating to see these two fine machines pitted against one another during Germany's losing battle for Britain.

The Heinkel He 112 V10 coded D-IGSI seen from its rear port side. Heinkel AG kept modifying their basic He 112 prototype fighter with the hope that the *RLM* would soon come to realize the obvious: that the *He 112* was a better machine than the *Bf 109*. They didn't. The *He 112 V10* shown in this photo differed from earlier prototypes; among other changes, it has a rear cockpit canopy to provide better all around vision.

The He 112 V10 seen nose on undergoing testing. This machine does not appear to have any cannon installed, certainly no German manufacturer at the time was producing a propeller hub mounted cannon compatible with the *Schwarz* three-bladed propeller.

The He 112 V10 giving a nice view of its fuselage nose-mounted oval radiator.

Focke-Wulf's entry in the RLM fighter design competition...its Fw 159 coded D-INGA. Kurt Tank and his aircraft design associates presented a machine with a braced parasol wing and a highly complicated main gear retraction system.

The Jumo 210C inverted 60° Vee 12 cylinder engine capable of producing 600 horsepower for take-off. The 210 was a German copy of the *Rolls-Royce "Kestral"* engine, which they were building under license from *Rolls-Royce*.

The Fw 159, seen in this photograph from its starboard side, was rejected almost immediately by the RLM.

Arado's entry in the *RLM's* fighter design competition...their *Ar 80 V1* and coded *D-ILOH*. It was never seriously in the fighter competition due to its heavy weight and inadequate power, plus it carried a fixed landing gear with spatted wheel covers similar to the *Junkers Ju 87* "*Stuka*." This machine never had a chance, and one has to wonder just what were the aircraft design folks back at *Arado* thinking when they submitted this design prototype to be Germany's next front line fighter?

Poor quality photos featuring a nose port side and full front view of Walter Blum's fighter design failure....the Ar 80 V1.

The Messerschmitt Bf 109 V13 featuring its nose starboard side view. This is the machine with its specially boosted *Daimler-Benz 600Ao* engine providing about 1,400 horsepower. *Carl Francke*, a Rechlin test pilot, won the Climb and Dive Competition at the 4th International Military Aircraft Competition, Zürich-Dübendorf, Switzerland, with the *Bf 109 V13*. With this victory, world governments took notice. The item on the ground in front of the propeller appears to be that portion of the upper fuselage cowling between the windscreen and engine.

Left to right: Carl Francke, Willy Messerschmitt, and General Erhard Milch. Milch is shaking Francke's hand in congratulations for winning the Climb and Dive Competitions in July 1937, in just a little over two minutes. World governments had never seen anything like it before, and Germany was gloating over the victory for *NAZISM*.

The Dornier Do *17* MV1 (actually the re-powered Do 17 V8). This re-engined machine put on a demonstration at the 4th International Military Airplane competition in July 1937 in Switzerland with a pair of specially boosted *Daimler-Benz DB 600Ao* engines providing an estimated 1,400 horsepower each. Observers were not told that this *Do 17MV1* was a one-of-a-kind machine built only for the 4ᵗʰ International Military Airplane competition. This machine attained a forward speed of 284 mph [458 km/h] verse the standard production *Do 17* speed of only 220 mph [354 km/h]. With this performance observers were really impressed, because the *Do17 MV1* was faster than most European fighters. General Erhard Milch was the copilot during this demonstration flight.

On 13 September 1935, American aircraft designer and manufacturer Howard Hughes flew his own Hughes H-1 Racer (NR-258Y) to an FAI air land speed record of 352.391 mph [567.115 km/] at Santa Anna, California. *Hughes* and America would go on to hold the record for almost two years.

A poor quality photograph featuring the starboard side of the specially boosted twin-engined Dornier Do 17M V1 bomber, which awed observers at the July 1937 4ᵗʰ International Military Aircraft Competition in Switzerland with level speeds (284 mph or 458 km/h) higher than most single engine fighters in Europe. *Dr. Josef Goebbels* ordered this machine so he could strike fear in the hearts of European nations that *NAZI* Germany was, indeed, the world's strongest and fastest air force.

Left to right: Fritz Wendel, unknown, Dr.-Ing. Hermann Wurster, Kaden, and Robert Lusser. It is 11 November 1937. These men, all from Messerschmitt AG, are congratulating *Wurster* after he took away *Howard Hughes'* crown as the fastest land pilot in the world. In the background is *Dr. Wurster's* mount...the record-breaking *Messerschmitt Bf 109 V13*.

The Enzian, a ground-to-air launched anti-aircraft missile (meaning "gentian," or that family of red, blue, white, and yellow flowers) developed by *Messerschmitt AG's Dr.-Ing. Hermann Wurster. Wurster* was thinking of the yellow gentian with its bitter root. The missile was launched on a metal ramp powered by four jettisonable solid fuel booster rockets. Upon clearing the launch, the *Enzian's* bi-fuel liquid rocket engine became active, with its booster rockets dropping away. The first launching of *Dr. Wurster's Enzian* was in August 1944. It reached a reported altitude of 49,212 feet [15,000 meters].

Dr.-Ing. Wurster's "Enzian" ground launched anti-aircraft missile mounted on a Flak 8.8 centimeter launching ramp. Wurster designed the missile to use the widely available Flak projectile launcher. The "Enzian" was controlled through the use of the ground-based radar "Würzberg-Riese" remote-control guidance system, which had been established for the night fighters.

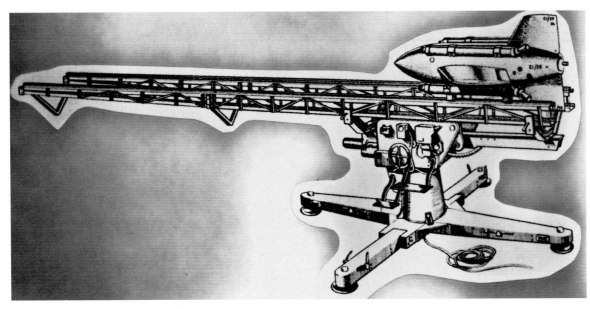

A pen and ink drawing of the "Enzian" on its Flak 8.8 centimeter projectile launching ramp.

The Heinkel He 100 V1 shown here without paint, national markings, or code numbers. It was first flown on 22 January 1938, and later, in March 1938, was sent to E-Stelle Rechlin for further testing. This machine's engine was cooled by wing surface evaporation, and while at Rechlin was test flown by *General Ernest Udet* to an unofficial *FAI* Absolute World Air Speed Record of 394.2 mph, thus bettering another unofficial world air speed record held by the Italian *Niclot* by more than 50 mph.

The Heinkel AG senior staff collected in front of the He 100 V2 coded D-IUOS. Left to right: Technical Director Josef Köhler; Chief of Construction *Schwärzler*; Chief Project Engineer *Siegfried Günter*; pilot and chief of the RLM's Technical Department, *General Ernst Udet*; Professor Ernst Heinkel; and *Dr.-Ing. Hertel*.

The He 100 V2 coded D-IVOS. Ernst Udet set a world's land air speed record of 394.2 mph over a 60 mile course on 6 June 1938.

The He 100 V2 coded *D-IUOS* flown by *General Ernst Udet* on *Whit* Sunday 6 June 1938 when he established the unofficial world air speed record of 394.2 mph in the 60 mile [100 kilometer], beating the unofficial world air speed record of the Italian *Breda* in a *Ba 88* by 50 mph. This machine was later designated the *He 112U...''U'* for *Udet*, by *Josef Goebbels*. In the background appears a *He 114* seaplane.

This is how Ernst Udet viewed himself after setting the record-breaking 60 mile [100 kilometer] closed course...dripping wet and shaking hands with Ernst Heinkel due to the *He 100 V2*'s wing surface evaporation cooling system. *Udet* was an accomplished cartoonist and enjoyed doing caricatures of himself and others. *Udet* was completely surprised after learning that he had just made a record-setting test flight and setting a new world's air speed record!

Walter Günter: 8 December 1899 to 21 September 1937. He loved the fast life: fast aircraft, cars, driving, and good living in general. Why be normal?

The two top Heinkel AG test pilots: Gerhard Nitschke and Hans Dieterle.

The He 100 V3 coded D-ISVR and with fake Luftwaffe markings suggesting that it was an operational aircraft...but it was all a lie. Nevertheless, this machine was very advanced, with its low drag windscreen and so on. It was lost in September 1938 at Warnemünde when *Gerhard Nitschke* found that one of the undercarriage oleo struts would not extend out of its wheel well. *Nitschke* bailed out of the crippled machine only to hit the tail plane. He was not seriously injured, suffering a broken collar bone, however, that prevented him from piloting the *He 100 V8.*

Flugkapitän Hans Dieterle seen in the He 100 V8, which is powered by an estimated 1,800 to 2,000 horsepower DB 601. Dieterle would fly this machine at 463.92 mph on 30 March 1939 to an air speed record. Seen in the lower right hand corner is a ground-man dressed in black coveralls assisting *Dieterle* get into the *V8* machine started and running.

Twenty-four year old Hans Dieterle and his He 100 V8 appear to be ready for take-off at Heinkel AG facilities at Oranienburg, because all ground support equipment and the men in the black coveralls have moved away.

Hans Dieterle gives the camera man a smile as he peers out from the starboard side of his He 100 V8. Notice that although the aluminum skin is unpainted it has been given plenty of body filler to seal up joints to make the surface more aerodynamically smooth.

The He 100 V8 coded D-IDGH which gave Germany her first FAI Absolute Land Air Speed Record. Shown at Heinkel AG facilities Oranienburg.

Hans Dieterle being given a bear hug by Heinkel AG Technical Director Josef Köhler after Dieterle won the absolute world air speed record on 30 March 1939. This machine appears to have been coded He+B? Notice, too, that the vertical rudder on this machine has been painted all black?

A group photo of many of the ground crewmen responsible for Hans Dieterle's record-breaking flight. Hans Dieterle, wearing goggles, is sitting on the V8's starboard wing. Heinkel AG's Technical Director, *Josef Köhler*, wearing the dark leather long coat and beret, along with *Frau Köhler* in the fur coat, seen next to her husband.

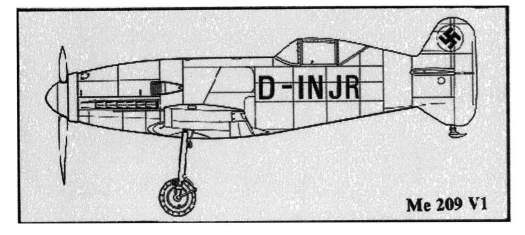

A pen and ink drawing of the Me 209 V1 coded D-INJR featuring its port side. Courtesy of Monogram's Messerschmitt O-Nine Gallery.

Three of the fastest aircraft racer pilots in the world in mid 1939: left, Italy's Francesco Agello, Heinkel AG's Hans Dieterle, and Gerhard Nitschke.

Josef Goebbels and son are seen here smiling at *Adolf Hilter* and one of his so-called "one dish meals." The entire meal was cooked up in the large pot seen at the bottom of the photograph. It was *Goebbels* who had to have a *Bf 109* hold the *FAI's* Absolute Land Air Speed Record, because how else would he be able to tell world governments that Germany possessed the world's fastest fighter?

The real *Me 209 V1* machine and featuring its port side. Notice its extra long oleo struts to accommodate its large diameter propeller.

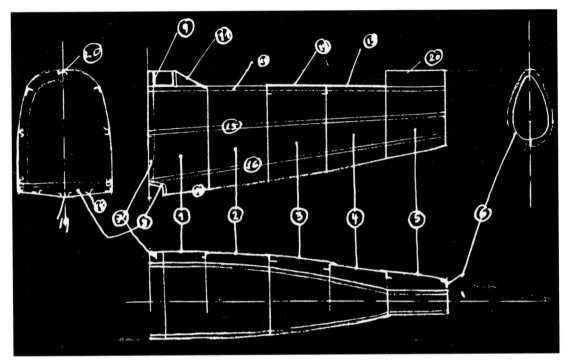

A hand-drawn diagram of the Me 209's aft fuselage with bulkheads and stringers.

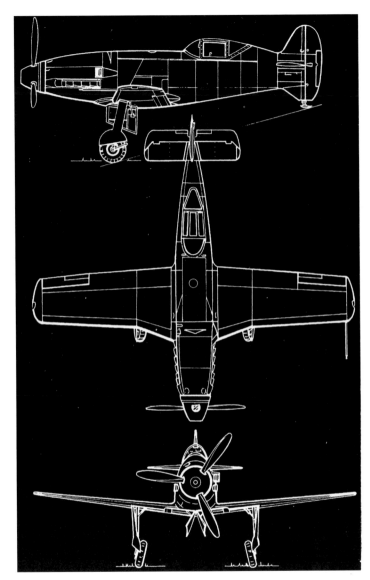

A pen and ink three view drawing of the Me 209 V1.

The Me 209 V1 as seen from its tail starboard side. Notice the raw dark and light aluminum panels covering the fuselage.

A pen and ink drawing of the Me 209 V1's port side nose surface featuring its propeller, engine exhaust stubs, air intake vent, port side extended landing gear, and wheel cover. Drawing by *Günter Sengfelder*.

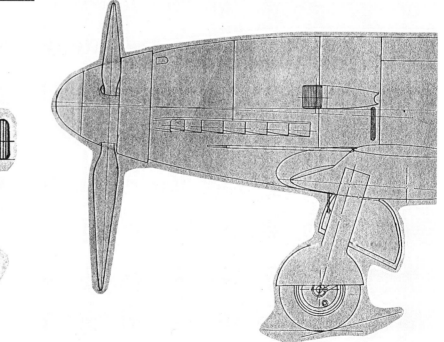

A see through pen and ink drawing of the front of the Me 209 V1's specially boosted DB 601 ANJ *60° Vee 12 cylinder engine. Drawing by Günter Sengfelder.*

A see through pen and ink drawing of the Me 209 V1's port side without its aluminum skin, featuring its specially boosted DB 601 ANJ *60° Vee 12 cylinder engine providing an estimated 1,800 horsepower. Drawing by Günter Sengfelder*.

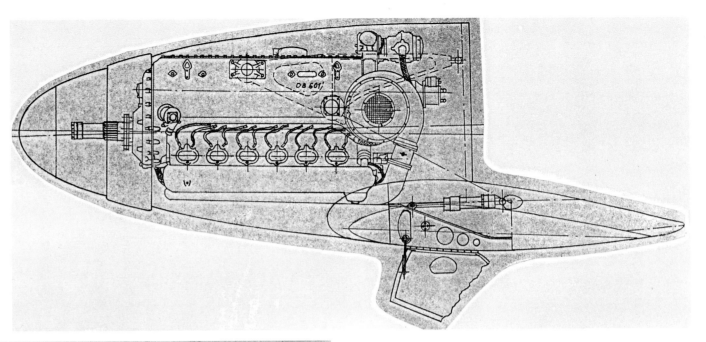

Below: This is a port side view of the specially boosted *DB 601 ANJ* engine placed in the *Me 209 V1*, which produced an estimated 1,800 horsepower for speed record-breaking attempts. Otherwise, this engine was a straight-forward 12 cylinder inverted 60° *Vee* and chiefly distinguished for its gasoline injection system. Notice, too, its metal pipe engine supporting cantilever arms to save weight compared to the conventional *Bf 109s* which used a forged alloy cantilever arm.

- displacement - 2,069 cubic inches [33.9 liters]
- control - single throttle control from pilot's cockpit
- spark plugs - two per cylinder fitted on the outside of the block
- magneto - *Bosch* twin unit *ZM.12 B.R.4* type
- lubrication - gear-type pressure on pump delivering through wire-wound filter—main oil supply led by drilled passages in crankcase to main bearings—scavenged oil drains from front to rear to cam case coverings, in each of which is gear-type pump
- exhaust - ejector type stubs
- supercharger - centrifugal type driven through hydraulic coupling—coupling impeller driven through 10.39 to 1 gearing from crankshaft
- auxiliaries - mounted on gear box at rear include: gear-type fuel pump, 24 volt 1,500 watt electrical generator, swashplate-driven six-plunge hydraulic pump (alternatively vacuum pump), centrifugal coolant pump, and hand/electric inertia starter
- dimensions: length 67.5 inches [1.714 meters], width 29.1 inches [0.739 meters], height 40.5 inches [1.028 meters], weight about 2,002 pounds [910 kilograms]

A dapper-looking Dr.-Ing. Hermann Wurster in suit and tie stands at the Me 209 V1's port side wing root of that "little monster," as he lovingly called it. The small oval opening on the wing's wing root by *Dr. Wurster's* right hand is the air intake for the steam to water condensing radiator. Another opening was on the opposite side.

A view of the Me 209 V1's port side fuselage at the Polish Air Museum in Kracow, Poland. The white, round object to the left of the photo is the *V1's* water tank, holding about 50 gallons.

The Me 209 V1's steam to water condensing radiator. This radiator was located in the fuselage about at the wing's trailing edge. Spit flaps could be raised or lowered to allow more cooling via increased air flow as the *DB 601 ANJ* engine's water temperature rose during its 30 to 35 minutes running time.

A close-up view of the spit flaps and their articulation rods on the Me 209 V1's steam to water condensing radiator.

The Me 209 V1's engine-less fuselage. Seen here are its pipe-like oleo struts without wheels. Hard to see, but at top center of the photo can be seen the aluminum alloy pipe cantilever *DB 601 ANJ* engine supports. Finally, one can see the wing's main spar aft the wing's leading edge.

The wing's main spar in the Me 209 V1 as viewed from below and from the front. Port is to the left in the photo and starboard to the right.

Static stress testing of the Me 209 V1's wing. Shown is the *V1's* starboard side. Wooden blocks have been placed under the wing to which weights will be placed later in an effort to see if the main spar can sustain the design loading, and if so, how much more before the wing buckles.

The starboard wing on the Me 209 V1 following its static weight testing. Notice that at the leading edge about where the oleo strut is mounted, the wing has buckled due to progressively heavier loads placed on it.

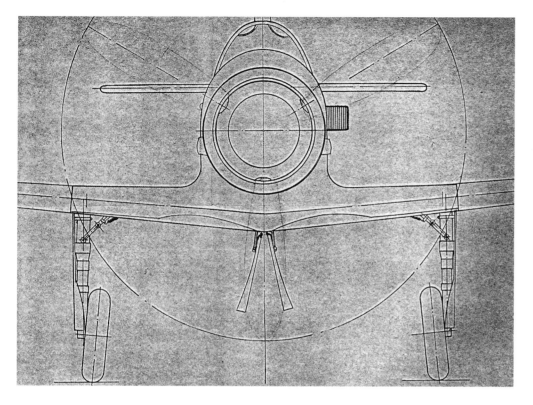

A pen and ink drawing featuring the Me 209's oleo struts, main wheels, and inner wheel cover doors. This drawing shows the Me 209 V4 landing gear. Except for the oleo struts—their length primarily—everything else is the same as it was in the *Me 209 V1*. Drawing by *Günter Sengfelder*.

A view of the Me 209 V1's main wheels as seen from this starboard nose view. Scale model and photograph by *Günter Sengfelder*.

A pen and ink drawing featuring the Me 209's main wheels and inner wheel cover doors. Its port side gear is fully extended, while the starboard side is fully retracted. Drawing by *Günter Sengfelder*.

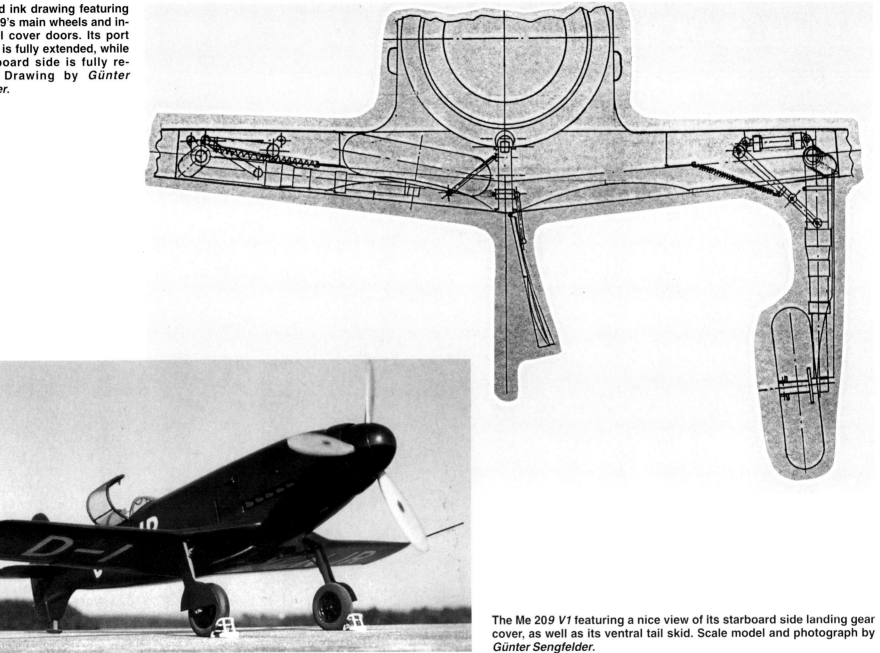

The Me 209 V1 featuring a nice view of its starboard side landing gear cover, as well as its ventral tail skid. Scale model and photograph by *Günter Sengfelder*.

The Me 209 V1's forward center section wing featuring both main wheels fully retracted. Notice the compactness of the fully retracted gear. Behind the wheel wells are water circulation pumps and pipes circulating the water to and from its condensing radiator.

The under side of the Me 209 V1's wing featuring the starboard wheel well, in particular the oleo strut's space when retracted. The starboard's oleo strut had not yet been installed when this photograph was taken.

A close-up of the mounting hardware for attaching the Me 20*9 V1's* port side oleo strut and retraction arm.

The Me 209 V1 port side oleo strut and retraction arm as seen from below with the oleo strut attached to the main spar.

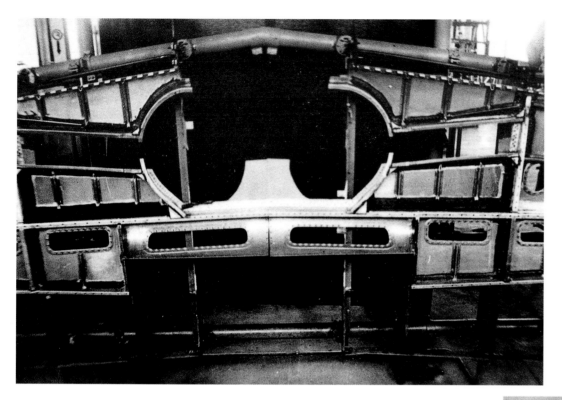

The underside of the upper surface of a Me 209's wing. Quite possibly, this photo shows the V4's wing with its shorter oleo struts, and numerous round and rectangular ports, nonetheless, this photo shows the relative position of the empty wheel wells prior to the installation of the oleo struts and wheel assemblies.

A close up of the Me 209 V1's oleo strut (to the far right in the photo) and its retraction arm and attachment to the main spar.

The hinged open starboard landing gear cover on the Me 209 *V1*. Notice the tank above the wheel well with assorted pipes and plumbing coming and going from its steam to water condensing radiator.

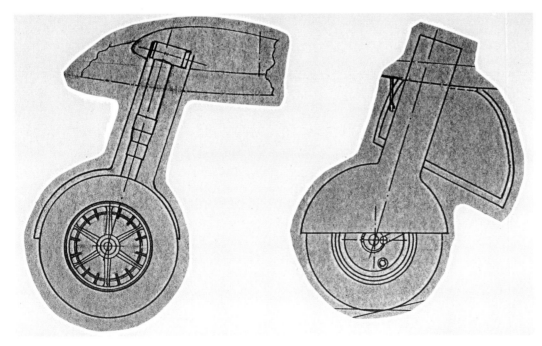

A pen and ink drawing of the Me 209 V4's main gear with covers. To the left is the inside main wheel and oleo strut attachment point. To the right is the outside view of the port side main wheel featuring the landing gear cover, and behind it, the hinged portion hanging down from the undersurface of the wing. Drawing by *Günter Sengfelder*.

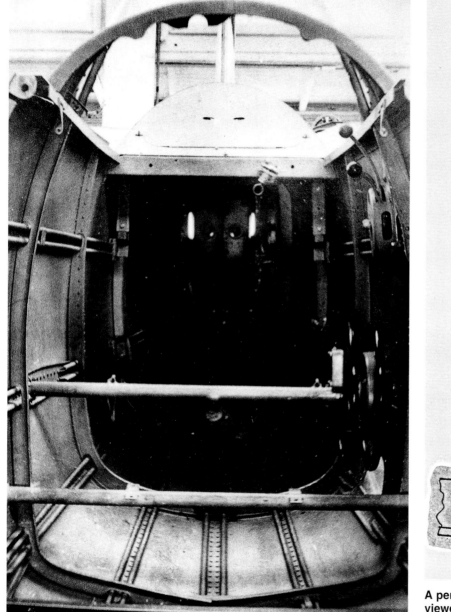

A view of the Me 209 V1's unfinished interior fuselage looking aft the cockpit, featuring its strings and bulkheads.

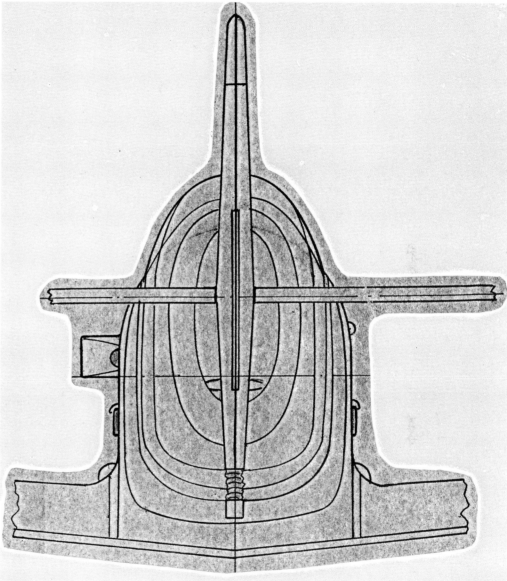

A pen and ink drawing of the *Me 209 V1's* increasing diameter of the fuselage bulkheads as viewed from the machine's tail plane. Drawing by *Günter Sengfelder*.

A view of the Me 209 V1 from its rear and looking forward. Scale model and photograph by *Günter Sengfelder*.

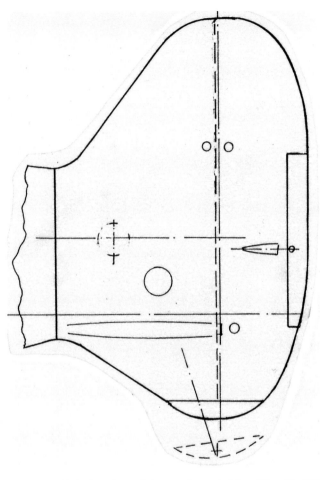

A pen and ink drawing of the starboard side of the *Me 209 V1's* vertical/ventral stabilizer without the elevator and tail skid. Drawing by *Günter Sengfelder*.

The Me 209 V1 and featuring its tail plane assembly and tail skid. Scale model and photograph by *Günter Sengfelder*.

A close-up of the Me 209 V1 in flight. It is reported that when this machine flew a steady stream of steam followed in its wake. Notice its tail skid mounted on the ventral stabilizer.

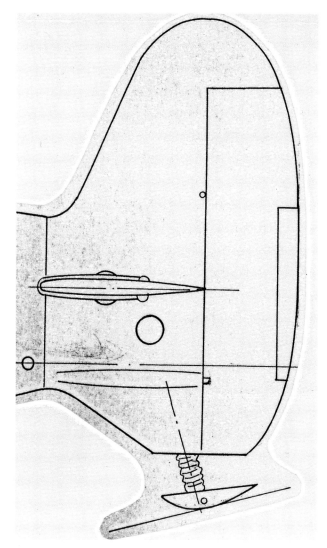

A pen and ink drawing of the Me 209 V1's starboard side vertical/ventral stabilizer with its elevator and tail skid included. Drawing by Günter Sengfelder.

The Me 209 V1 is photographed making a low pass over what appears to be picket fencing.

A sequence of photos featuring the *Me 209 V1* in flight. In this photo the *Me 209 V1* is seen heading left from right. *FAI* rules in place in 1939 required the man and machine to complete two passes over a closed 1.86 mile course in each direction in attempting a new air speed record.

Above Right: The Me 209 V1 has reversed itself, apparently after completing a pass in one direction. It is now heading back to the right from left to complete this pass...hence two passes in each direction.

Right: A freight train pulling a number of freight cars is photographed passing one of the check points used by the pilot of the Me 209 V1 earlier in the day to establish a new FAI Absolute Land Air Speed Record.

A public relations photograph passed around by Dr. Josef *Goebbels' Reich's* Ministry of Propaganda. During its flight tests, the *Me 209 V1's* aluminum panels were unpainted. Later, the air speed record-breaking machine was sent to the *Berlin Museum*. Before it was, however, Messerschm*itt AG* was instructed by *Josef Goebbels* to paint the machine a dark blue with white code letters. After the *Me 209 V1* had its new paint job, *Willy Messerschmitt* and pilot *Fritz Wendel* posed for a series of photographs. It is not known to this author why *Goebbels* chose dark blue and white lettering.

Fritz Wendel in the cockpit of the Me 209 V1 appears to be chatting with Willy Messerschmitt.

With the photographic session apparently over, *Willy Messerschmitt* extends his hand to assist *Fritz Wendel* out of the *Me 209 V1's* cockpit.

Left to right: Fritz Wendel looking dapper with his ascot tie around his neck, and Willy Messerschmitt.

Willy Messerschmitt, Fritz Wendel in a tuxedo, and *Adolf Hitler*. They are celebrating Germany's *FAI* Absolute World Air Speed Record captured from *Ernst Heinkel* by their so-called *Bf 109* (also known as the *Me 209 V1*).

*Adolf Hitler, Albert Speer, and Martin Bormann, who was no friend of Ernst Heinkel, are seen inspecting a construction project po*st *assassination attempt on* Hitler's *life.*

Awards day at the Nuremburg Partei Rally on 1 September 1939. Left to right: Dr. Josef Goebbels, Adolf Hitler, Ernst Heinkel, Willy Messerschmitt (shaking hands with *Hitler*), *Ferdinand Porsche*, and *Fritz Todt*.

Air speed record-breaking pilots at a 1939 RLM ceremony: Flugkapitän Fritz Wendel (Me 209 V1 - 469.2 mph on 26 April 1939), Flugkapitän Hans Dieterle (He 100 V8 - 463.9 mph on 30 March 1939), Italian *Captain Francesco Agello* (*Mc-72* - 440.7 mph on 23 October 1934), *General Ernst Udet* (*He 100 V2* - 394.4 mph on 5 June 1938), and *Dr.-Ing. Hermann Wurster* (*Bf 109 V13* - 380.1 mph on 11 November 1937).

The same group of five air speed record-breaking pilots as seen in the above photo, but lined up in a different sequence: Hermann Wurster, Fritz Wendel, Francesco Agello, Ernst Udet, and Hans Dieterle.

The remains of the Me 209 V1 at the Polish Air Museum, Kracow, Poland, and featuring its port side. It appears that only the fuselage aft the DB 601 ANJ engine exists. The cylindrical white item to the left in the photo is the machine's 48 to 60 gallon cooling water tank. The Daimler-Benz engine was returned to Daimler-Benz and a wooden mockup was placed in the Me 209 V1 at the Berlin Air Museum. This author does not know what heppened to its wings. Courtesy Paul Nann, Military Aircraft Photo Gallery.

A split image of the Me 209 V1. To the right of the split in the photo is that portion of the Me 209 V1 which exists today at the Polish Air Museum. To the left of the split is that portion missing.

A close-up of the Me 209 V1's port side fuselage at the Polish Air Museum, Kracow, Poland. The machine's windscreen is gone, as well as its entire cockpit canopy. *See pp 65-80 for color photographs of this Me 209 V1.*

An overhead view of the Me 209 V1's fuselage. It appears in the middle of the photograph and is identified by the round port hole forward the windscreen frame.

A close-up of the Me 209 V1's current cockpit interior featuring its instrument panel. The pipe-like item to the right in the cockpit with the rectangular shape on its top end is the machine's control stick. Most, if not all of the *V1's* instruments are gone from its wooden instrument panel.

Ernst Heinkel and Ernst Udet. Udet had the unpleasant job of telling his long-time friend that although Fritz Wendel had only broken the He 100 V8 absolute world air speed record by about 1.0 mile per hour, he would not be allowed to better Wendel's FAI-recognized air speed record. Dr. Goebbels had decreed no further attempts would be tolerated with the goal to break Wendel's record.

The unflappable Ernst Heinkel did not stay down for long. He had had his design engineers working on another pioneering aircraft project, and with his own money for several years prior...his single turbojet-powered He 178. The He 178 was the world's first turbojet-powered aircraft. Its propulsion came from a Heinkel AG centrifugal turbojet design known as the HeS 3B, producing 1,102 pounds of thrust. The maiden flight of the He 178 came on 27 August 1939 at Marienehe and was test flown by Flugkapitän Erich Warsitz, a former test pilot for the RLM at Rechlin, who was now working for Heinkel AG.

A pen and ink drawing of the port side of the Me 209 V2. Courtesy Monogram's Messerschmitt O-Nine Gallery.

A poor quality photo of the Me 209 V2 coded D-*IWAH werk numer 1186* under construction at *Messerschmitt AG* facilities Augsburg. Featured in this photo is the *Me 209 V2's* port side.

The Me 209 V2's tail assembly and featuring its vertical stabilizer's elevator trim tabs. This machine has the Halkenkruez (swastika) in red applied within a black band on the upper portion of the vertical stabilizer.

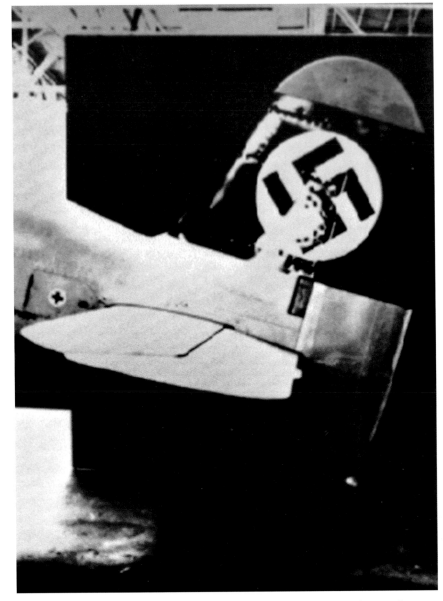

Me 209 V2's port side view of its tail assembly. Notice the "red cross" emergency symbol painted on the square access hatch forward the port elevator. This author is not sure what was placed in this hatch or for what emergency medical use it was to be used.

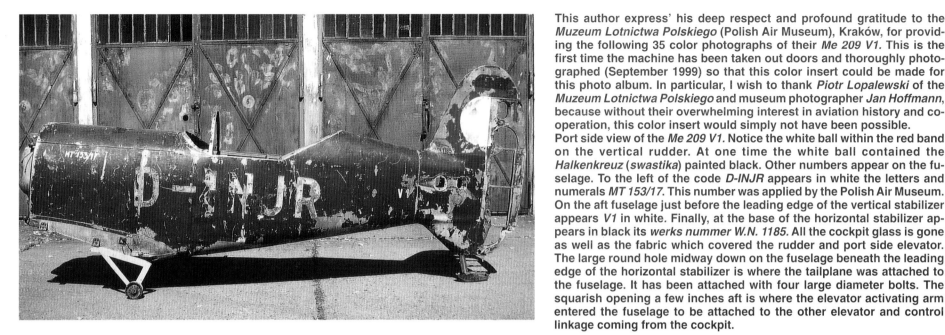

This author express' his deep respect and profound gratitude to the *Muzeum Lotnictwa Polskiego* (Polish Air Museum), Kraków, for providing the following 35 color photographs of their *Me 209 V1*. This is the first time the machine has been taken out doors and thoroughly photographed (September 1999) so that this color insert could be made for this photo album. In particular, I wish to thank *Piotr Lopalewski* of the *Muzeum Lotnictwa Polskiego* and museum photographer *Jan Hoffmann*, because without their overwhelming interest in aviation history and co-operation, this color insert would simply not have been possible.

Port side view of the *Me 209 V1.* Notice the white ball within the red band on the vertical rudder. At one time the white ball contained the *Halkenkreuz* (*swastika*) painted black. Other numbers appear on the fuselage. To the left of the code *D-INJR* appears in white the letters and numerals *MT 153/17*. This number was applied by the Polish Air Museum. On the aft fuselage just before the leading edge of the vertical stabilizer appears *V1* in white. Finally, at the base of the horizontal stabilizer appears in black its *werks nummer W.N. 1185*. All the cockpit glass is gone as well as the fabric which covered the rudder and port side elevator. The large round hole midway down on the fuselage beneath the leading edge of the horizontal stabilizer is where the tailplane was attached to the fuselage. It has been attached with four large diameter bolts. The squarish opening a few inches aft is where the elevator activating arm entered the fuselage to be attached to the other elevator and control linkage coming from the cockpit.

Starboard side view of the *Me 209 V1.* No letters or numbers appear on this side of the fuselage with the exception of its code *D-INJR*. The machine had been painted a dark blue. According to *Günter Sengfelder*, the *Me 209 V1's Daimler-Benz 601* high performance engine was taken back by *Daimler-Benz* after the record flight. Its fuselage aluminum panels were left unpainted before its record-breaking flight and the machine was painted a dark blue afterwards. The light rust color showing through today, where the blue had been, is its green primer paint.

Starboard side view of the *Me 209 V1's* wing root area. The dark colored flexible hose coming out of the fuselage is the wheel-brake's hydraulic hose. In the upper right-hand corner of the photo can be seen two metal lines. They are hydraulic lines for the cockpit gauges. The two rust-colored "L" brackets attached to fuselage side with four through bolts and a single large diameter hole in the bottom were used to help attach the wing to the fuselage. Note, too, the area of the fuselage directly above the black wheel on the dolly is a clamp with a threaded bolt. This is one of the means used to join that nose portion of fuselage containing fuel and water tanks, to the cockpit section of the fuselage.

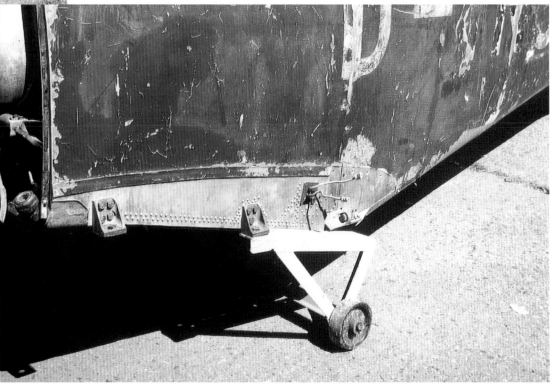

Port side view of the *Me 209 V1's* wing root. In addition to the two rust-colored "L" brackets, the port side has two small diameter metal tubing coming out through the wing root. They are hydraulic lines for the undercarriage extension/retraction system. To the far left and about half way up the photo at the base of the fuselage, can be seen a large diameter metal connection. It is the lower port engine mount. The bracket above it is the mounting tube for the machine's water tank.

A view of the *Me 209 V1's* complete horizontal tail plane and in surprisingly good condition although the starboard tail plane has suffered some damage and the port side fabric covering is gone. Between the port and starboard tailplane pieces can be seen the large diameter mounting plate. Aft the mounting piece can be seen the elevator's activating arm.

A full view of the total remains of the *Me 209 V1* in the Polish Air Museum as seen from directly behind. Notice that the starboard side elevator still has its fabric, however, suffers a damaged tip. The metal cowling seen to the left of the photograph attaches to the underside of the fuselage forward the leading edge of the wing and beneath the *Daimler-Benz 601* engine. Of course, the forward section of the fuselage belonging to this cover is missing as is the engine and propeller. The original *DB 601* engine was returned to *Daimler-Benz* after the machine established a new world's air speed record. Later, a conventional *DB 601* with a wooden propeller was installed in the machine for display purposes. Their whereabouts today are unknown.

The port side elevator for the *Me 209 V1* lying on the concrete as viewed from above and behind. Pieces of the fabric-covered elevator can still be seen on the rudder structure.

The starboard side elevator for the *Me 209 V1* lying on the concrete as viewed from above and behind.

A direct head on view of the *Me 209 VI's* fuselage looking aft to the vertical stabilizer. The aluminum tank, containing water, was located directly behind the *Daimler-Benz 601*. The large diameter port, minus its cover, leads to the high octane gasoline fuel tank.

A close-up view of the *Me 209 V1's* aluminum insulated "*cool stuff*" tank, its hold-down metal straps, and plumbing. Notice to the far left and about center in the photo can be seen a bundle of cable ends which then lead back into the cockpit. To the far right and center in the photo can be seen an attachment device for the fuselage side cowling. At the bottom of the fuselage can be seen two large diameter holes. This is where the cantilever engine mount's lower arms were bolted on to the fuselage. Where the port upper arm bolted onto the fuselage can be seen just above the "*cool stuff*" tank. It is seen as a large round hole in the upper right side of the photograph. The long dark cable appearing on the left side of the "*cool stuff*" tank with a connection at its end is the cable coming from the engine to the cockpit for the mechanically-driven engine revolution counter.

The fuselage top metal cowling/cover forward the *Me 209 V1* cockpit windscreen has been removed showing what's beneath as seen in this starboard side view. The first aluminum tank, to the far right of the photograph is for the "*cool stuff*" coolant followed by the machine's high octane gasoline fuel tank. The fabric-covered area forward the cockpit's windscreen is access to the flight instruments and the fabric was placed there to protect the instrument's electrical connections.

This is an interesting photo. A close-up photo of the *Me 209 V1's* "*cool stuff*" and high octane gasoline tank compartment. This area holds two individual tanks, the two metal hold-down straps cover the "*cool stuff*" tank. Notice the large gasoline filler port to the left in the photograph. The gasoline tank was riveted securely to the fuselage. In the upper portion of the photograph beyond the gasoline filler can be seen the machine's throttle linkage. It takes curious route coming out from the port side of the cockpit across the top of the gasoline tank where stops and attaching to a rod crossing over the gasoline tank to the starboard side. A this point it disappears down between the two tanks and the linkage then extends on to the *DB 601* engine. Appearing in the lower portion of the photograph (starboard side) are a collection of cables. The cable appearing wire wrapped is an electrical line while the blue-colored line is a hydraulic line. Moving forward of the gasoline filler port can be seen a yellow-colored line. This is the gasoline fuel line to the *DB 601*. In the upper right hand corner of the photo are various wires. They are electrical connections.

A port side view of the *Me 209 V1* with the only other known piece of the machine to have survived...its aluminum nose/engine lower fuselage cowling. It is shown in this photograph about where it would be located if the engine and propeller were attached.

The aluminum "*cool stuff*" - gasoline tank cowling/cover. To the left of the photo is the forward end and notice that the coolant cover states "*Kühlstoff*" or "*cool stuff*." This coolant fluid was composed of 80% water, 48.5% glykol, and 1.5% Shell #39 oil. The cowling's metal cover for the high octane gasoline access port has been lost.

The port side view of the under engine cowling/cover shown placed on its aft end. Notice the long, steel rod used to aline and help secure the cowling. There were four such long, steel rods on this cowling, one at each corner.

The starboard side view of the under engine cowling/cover shown placed on its aft end.

The reverse side of the under engine cowling/cover shown placed on its aft end.

The inside appearance of the cowling covering the underside of the *Daimler-Benz 601* racing engine. It appears to be in remarkably good condition. The long rods at each corner are needed to go between the exhaust stacks and reach the upper cowling where it is secured. The circular item seen is a vent, allowing the escapement of water vapor/steam from the engine's cooling system.

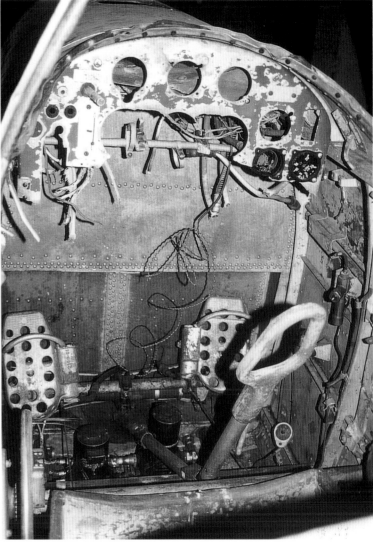

Starboard side view of the *Me 209 V1's* windowless cockpit. The metal frame with its two hand grips support the windscreen. The remains of the machine's instrument panel can be seen through the cockpit canopy frame.

The *Me 209 V1's* cockpit, instrument panel, foot rudder pedals, and control stick as seen from the port side. The wires and tubing hanging down were at one time attached to the missing instruments and perhaps have been taken by souvenir hunters over the past sixty years. Otherwise, the cockpit area of the *Me 209 V1* appears to be in relatively good condition. Notice that no glass at all appears in the metal framework.

A close-up view of the *Me 209 V1's* foot rudder pedals, "*cool stuff*" pumps, and related tubing, all mounted on the cockpit floor. The yellow tube to the far right in the photo is a drainage line from the gasoline tank filler. The two pumps located on the cockpit floor, between the rudder pedals, are the "*cooling stuff*" pumps. Underneath the floorboard, they were located between the engine, wings, and "*cool stuff*" tanks. Notice the green lines...green means that they contained coolant liquid.

A view of the *Me 209 V1's* cockpit as seen from its starboard side. The trim wheel, mounted between the fuselage wall and the pilot's seat, is seen as well as a second wheel for the landing flaps. The throttle (slide push-pull) lever, is mounted on the fuselage wall, above the trim wheels with a rod leading forward through the instrument panel. The end of this rod extends to the upper surface of the gasoline fuel tank and then on to the engine. In the bottom center of the photograph is the pilot's metal seat.

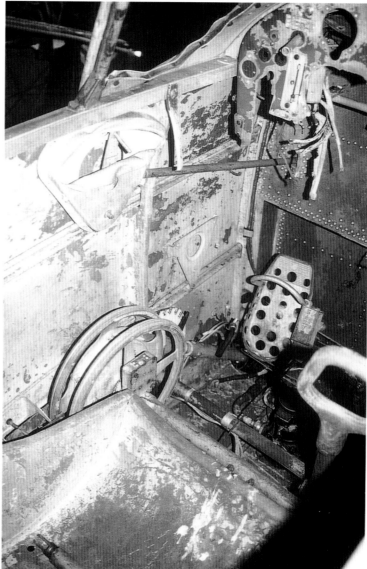

A view of the *Me 209 V1's* cockpit as seen from its port side. The only remaining instrument in the instrument panel is its fuel contents gauge reading up to (290 liters). Below the gauge, on the fuselage wall, can be seen a brass valve. It is the oxygen valve for controlling the flow of oxygen to the pilot's oxygen mask. To the right of the oxygen valve can be seen an open red-colored box. This box held electrical fuses or circuit breakers. Below the circuit breaker box to the left can be seen a pulley and steel cables. This was part of the emergency cockpit canopy jettison system. The red bracket below the circuit breaker box and to the right was a bracket holding a hand-held fire extinguisher.

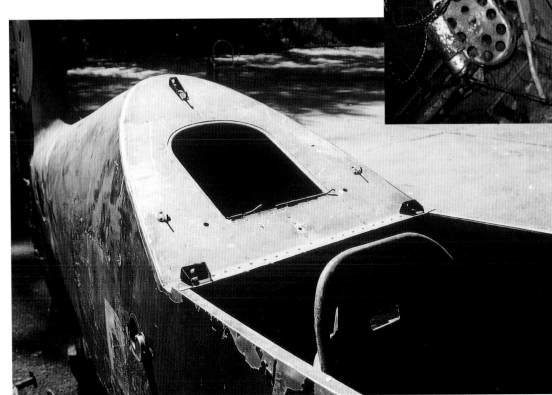

The rear cockpit-area of the *Me 209 V1* as seen from its starboard side. The large opening is an access port for the machine's alcohol tank. The top back of the pilot's seat can be seen in the lower right of the photograph. The small round opening on the fuselage seen in the bottom left of the photo is an electrical connection for the machine's 24 volt operating system.

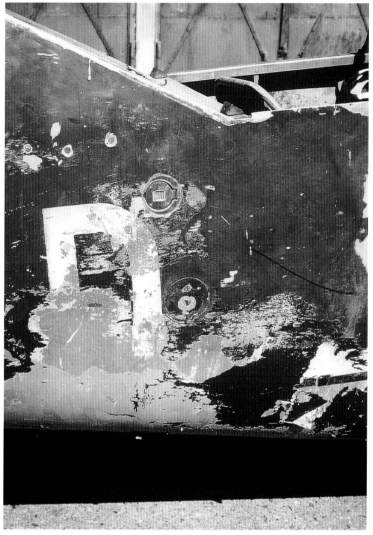

The rear cockpit-area of the *Me 209 V1* as seen from its port side. The three metal brackets were hold-down mountings for the rear part of the cockpit canopy. Notice that the area behind the access port has been illuminated by the flash camera. The pilot's seat back has suffered a gash on its starboard side coming from the air raid on the Berlin Aviation Museum where the machine had been on public display.

Direct side view of the aft cockpit of the *Me 209 V1* as seen from its starboard side. Two access ports are visible. The upper is an electrical receptacle (outlet) for taking an external 24 volt power line while the aircraft is on the ground. The purpose of the lower access port is unclear.

A view from the seat back access port into the aft area of the fuselage. The linkage seen here, above the jacking support bar, is for the elevators (top linkage) and for the rudder (lower linkage).

The pilot's cockpit seat and seat back. In the lower left corner of the photograph is the machine's triangular-like control stick handle.

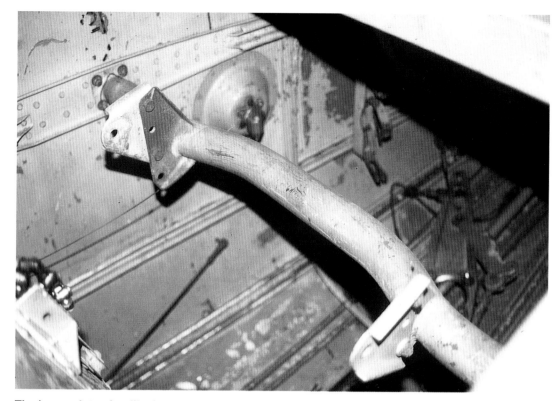

The heavy-duty pipe-like item reaching port to starboard is the pilot's seat back support bracket. The pilot's seat has been removed showing the bracket to which it would be bolted and a portion of its can be seen in the lower left hand corner of the photograph. The machine's 24 volt electrical receptacle (outlet) can be seen in the top center of the photograph, behind the seat back support. Rudder and elevator linkage can be seen in the right side of the photograph behind the seat back support.

The port side view of the *Me 209 V1's* tailplane section. The fabric has disappeared from the rudder but otherwise the tail assembly looks in very good condition for being in storage for over sixty years. The hydraulic metal tail skid appears to be in good condition as well. Notice the machine's *werks nummer* painted on the vertical fin...*W.N. 1185*. Two openings can be seen in the tail assembly. The first is where the vertical stabilizers are bolted on to the fuselage. The second opening is where the actuating arm moving the elevators enter the fuselage. There is no trace of the *Halkenkruez* (*swastika*) within the white ball where it once appeared having been painted over.

The starboard side view of the *Me 209 V1's* tailplane section. It is a mirror image of the port side except that it carries no *werks nummer*. The bulge in the ventral portion of the tail fin seen between the horizontal stabilizer and the metal tail skid was required to allow linkage sufficient space when moving the rudder.

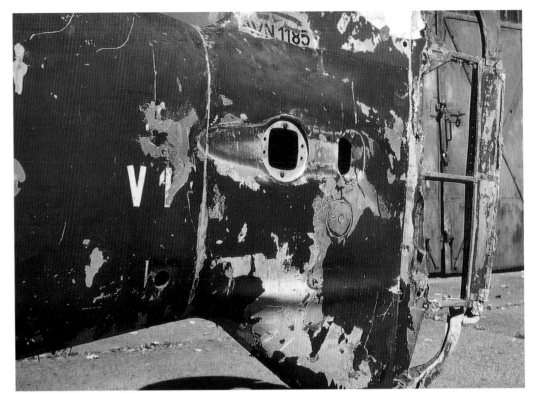

The port side view of the *Me 209 V1's* tail assembly. Notice the "*V1*" appearing just forward the tail assembly. The large diameter hole direct beneath the "*V1*" is a jacking or lifting point, that is, where the tail could be lifted up off the ground for maintenance.

A close-up of the *Me 209 V1's* port side tail assembly and featuring it faded red band going around the tail assembly and its fuselage blue paint job as well as its black hand painted *werks nummer*.

A view of the port side rudder showing that its fabric is long gone and showing, too, its internal aluminum framework. The ventral portion of the vertical stabilizer houses the hydraulically retracted metal tail skid. It was extended via compressed air and oil.

A close-up of the hydraulically retractable metal tail skid pad as seen from its port side. The skid pad was extended by compressed air and oil. Upon close inspection it appears to be in relatively good condition.

A piece of lower fuselage cowling for the Me 209 V2. This author does not know where it fits on the V2's fuselage.

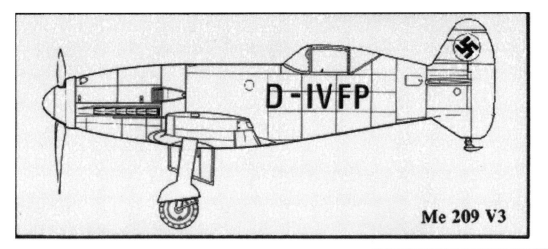

Me 209 V3

A pen and ink drawing of the *Me 209 V3's* port side fuselage and coded *D-IVFP*. Courtesy Monogram's *Messerschmitt O-Nine Gallery*.

A close-up of the Me 209 V3 featuring its rectangular air scoop funneling air back to the engine's radiator. The V3 is seen from its nose port side, and the purpose of this scoop was to eliminate the surface evaporative cooling of the *Me 209 V1* and *V2* and thereby allow the *DB* engine to operate cooler and stay within normal operating ranges. Notice that this machine's landing gear has no strut or wheel cover doors.

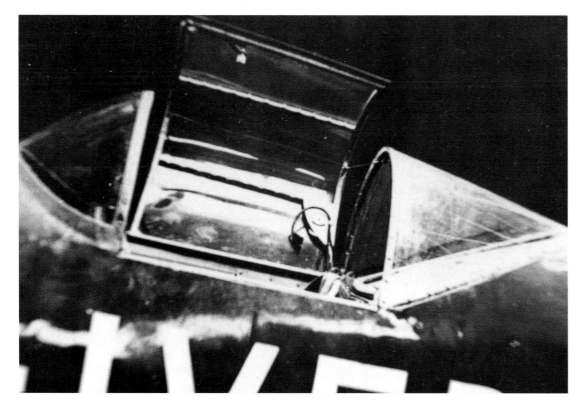

A port side close-up view of the Me 209 V3's cockpit and hinged cockpit canopy. The cockpit canopy and windscreens were not changed between the V1 and V4.

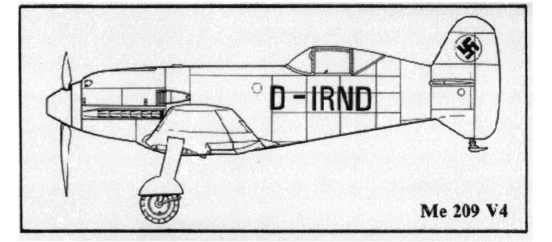

A pen and ink drawing of the port side of the Me 209 V4 coded *D-IRND*. It was this version which *Willy Messerschmitt* hoped would become a replacement for his aging *Bf 109*. After all the modifications, the *Me 209 V4* was worse than the aircraft it was supposed to replace. Courtesy Monogram's *Messerschmitt O-Nine Gallery*.

The Me 209 V4 after it was given its #14 civilian registration. It also carries the Halkenkruez and Balkenkruez. This photo gives a good view of the serpent's motif, showing its huge mouth really wide open.

The Me 209 V4 shown in flight. It was initially coded CE+BW with a Balkenkruez and Halkenkruez on its upper vertical stabilizer. Then, on about 20 September 1940 it was given the civilian registration #14. The serpents motif was added about the same and appears on both sides of the fuselage's nose.

A nose starboard side view of the Me 209 V4. It appears to have air movement testing items installed aft the wing's upper surface leading edges. The machine appears to have been flown as a tail dragger with its tail skid, that is, it seems to still lack a tail wheel.

The starboard side upper wing of the Me 209 V4 showing its automatic leading edge slot. This modification was made to help improve the machine's handling characteristics. The aluminum panels are unpainted, however, its code *D-IRND* appears in a dark color.

The in side of the upper surface of the starboard side wing for the Me 209 V4. This photo gives a good view of the leading edge slot and its articulation hardware. This author does not know the purpose of the several rectangular port holes in the wing's upper surface forward the trailing edge.

A view of the in side of the upper surface of the port side wing for the Me 209 V4.

A view of what appears to be the inner side of the upper surface wing panel on the Me 209 V4.

The inner side of the upper surface wing panel on the Me 209 V4. This author does not know the purpose of the large round port hole and why it was placed in this area.

What appears to be the inner side of the upper surface of the wing from the Me 209 V4. The trailing edge appears along the bottom of the photograph.

What appears to be the inside of the upper surface of the starboard side wing panel from the Me 209 V4. The line of rectangular ports appear to be forward the wing's trailing edge.

What appears to be the under surface of a wing panel of the *Me 209 V4* near its trailing edge. This author does not know the purpose of the long rectangular opening and whether or not it was covered with a plate prior to flight.

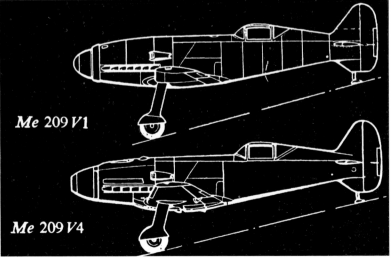

Me 209 V1

Me 209 V4

A pen and ink drawing of the Me 209 V1 and the V4's port side. The item of interest here is the length of the oleo strut on the main wheels. The *V4* has a longer oleo strut than did the *V1*.

A nose-on view of the Me 209 V4 coded D-IRND in its hangar and featuring its main landing gear and fuselage-mount gear cover doors.

A view of the Me 209 V4's starboard wing as seen from beneath. Left is toward its wing tip and right is the wing root area.

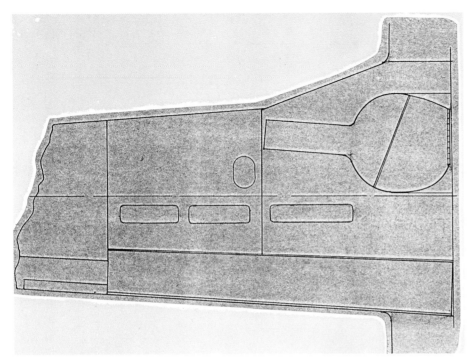

A pen and ink drawing of the under surface of the Me 209 V4's starboard wing with its several rectangular ports. Drawing by Günter Sengfelder.

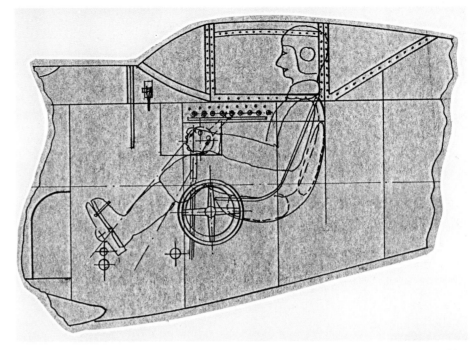

Pen and ink drawing of the pilot's cockpit in the Me 209 V4 fighter version and its other deviations as seen from its port side. Drawing by *Günter Sengfelder*.

Two views of the *Me 209 V4's* wheel wells. The photo on the left is the starboard side wheel well. At the bottom of the photo can be seen the fuselage-mounted hinged wheel cover. The photo on the right is the port side wheel well. To the far right of the photo can be seen the fuselage-mounted hinged wheel cover.

The Messerschmitt AG proposed replacement for its aging Bf 109 and challenger to the *Focke-Wulf Fw 190...the Me 209 V4. Shown here f*rom overhead is its starboard side with its painted on serpent (snake) emblem. Scale model by *Reinhard Roeser*.

The cockpit canopy of the Me 209 prototypes each lifted and opened to their starboard side...typical of the Messerschmitt Bf 109s. Scale model and photograph by *Günter Sengfelder*.

A near overhead view of the Me 209's overall planview, and featuring its open cockpit canopy which opened to starboard. Scale model and photograph by *Günter Sengfelder*.

Cockpit interior of the Me 209 V4 looking forward to the windscreen. The pilot's seat cushion can be seen at the bottom of the photo, control stick, rudder foot pedals, and instrument panel. Above the instrument panel can be seen the *Revi C/12D* gunsight, which was located between the two handgrip bars at the top of the windscreen.

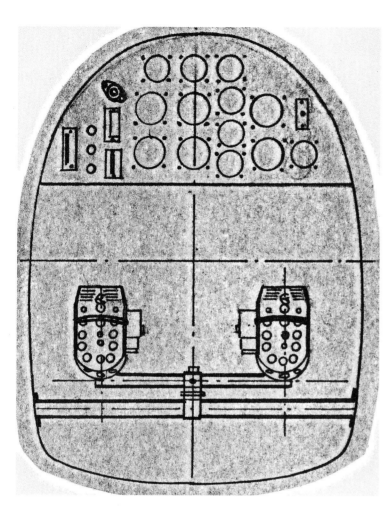

A pen and ink illustration of the instrument panel on the Me 209 V4 fighter prototype. Drawing by Günter Sengfelder.

A close up view of the starboard side cockpit instrument panel on the *Me 209 V4.* The *Revi C/12D* sight is visible at the top of the photograph, while the control stick and right foot rudder pedal are seen at the bottom center of the photo.

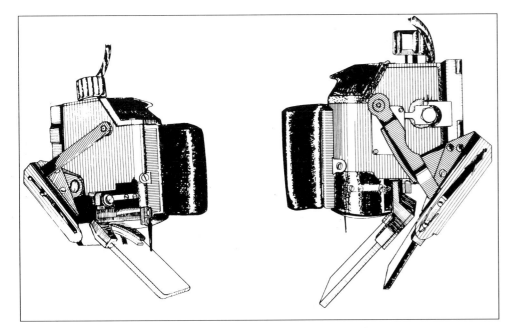

A pen and ink drawing of the Revi C/12D gunsight of the size and type installed in the Me 209 V4. Courtesy: Messerschmitt Bf 109 in Action by John Beaman, Jr., and *Jerry Campbell*. Squadron/Signal.

A port side view of the cockpit in the Me 209 V4 featuring the instrument panel, the Revi C/12D gun sight (at the top right-hand corner), control stick, and left rudder pedal.

A close-up of the Me 209 V4's pilot's rudder pedals in this modular fuselage component. Notice, too, the large circular disc in the center of the fuselage component. It is a backing plate for accessing the 1xMG 151 20 mm cannon firing through the propeller hub.

The Me 209 V4's starboard side and featuring its DB 601 metal alloy engine mount verses the metal pipe engine mount used on the Me 209 V1. At the top of the engine, back by the fire wall can be seen the *MG FF/M* cannon firing through the propeller hub.

The port side of the Me 209 V4 featuring its DB 601 engine.

One of the Me 209 V4's fuselage segments which housed the armament. It appears that this segment is being static weight tested. Notice how the *DB 601* metal alloy cantilever engine mounts have been rigged so to apply increasing pressure. To the left of center can be seen the access hole for the cannon firing through the propeller hub.

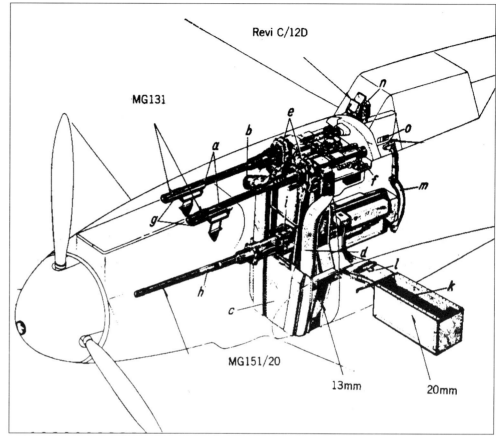

A pen and ink drawing of the nose of a Bf 109G and its armament, which would also be incorporated into the Me 209 V4...2x*MG 131*, plus a cannon firing through the propeller hub.

An overhead view of the Me 209 V4 and its fuselage between the cockpit instrument panel (right side of the photo) and the rear of the DB 601 engine (left side of the photo). Visible are three oxygen bottles mounted ahead of the instrument panel. Forward the oxygen bottles (the black area) is where the *MG FF/M* cannon was located. Each cannon shell was fired through the propeller hub.

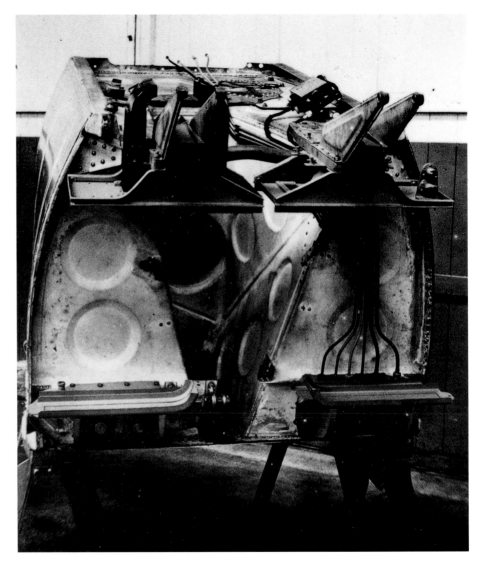

This photo shows the fuselage section containing the cannon firing through the propeller hub on the Me 209 V4. The upper most part can be seen two "U" shaped brackets which held one MG 131 cannon each.

Another view of the same fuselage modular section from the *Me 209 V4* as seen in the photo above.

A sequence of photos showing how Messerschmitt AG engineers designed the fuselage modular section in the Me 209 V4 out of stamped sheet metal which, when built up, will contain the cannon firing through the propeller hub. For orientation, that area of the piece with the large diameter hole faces the *Me 209 V4's* propeller.

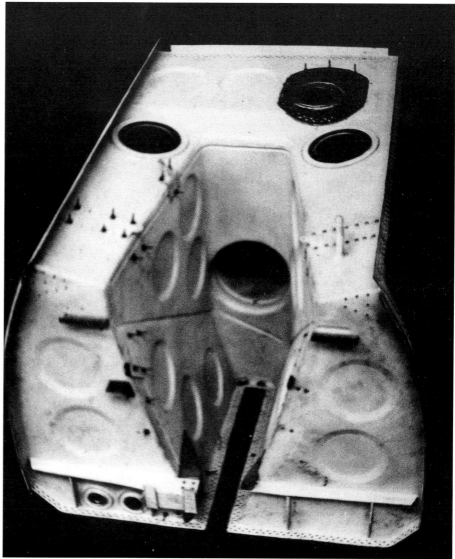

The fuselage modular section designed to hold the propeller cannon for the Me 209 V4 appears more built up in this photo. For orientation, that portion of the piece at the top of the photo faces the propeller, while the piece at the bottom of the photo forms a bulkhead between it and the cockpit.

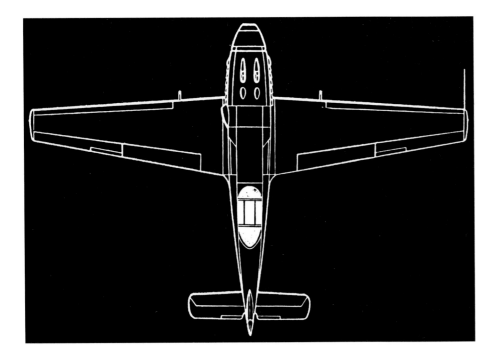

A pen and ink overall plan view drawing of the Me 209 V4. Notice the cannon ports for its 2xMG 131 cannons just aft the propeller.

The real thing. The *Me 209 V4*, showing its overall plan view.

The Me 209 V4 in military use was painted a cream , including markings such as the Halkenkruez and Balkenkruez. Scale model and photograph by *Reinhard Roeser*.

Willy Messerschmitt's proposed new fighter design based in part upon the Me 209 V4...the Me 209 V5. Scale model and photograph by Reinhard Roeser.

The Me 209 V5 prototype as seen from its starboard side.

Three of the several Me 209's left to right: the Me 2*09 V5*, the *Me 209 V1*, and the *Me 209 V4.* Scale models and photograph by *Reinhard Roeser.*

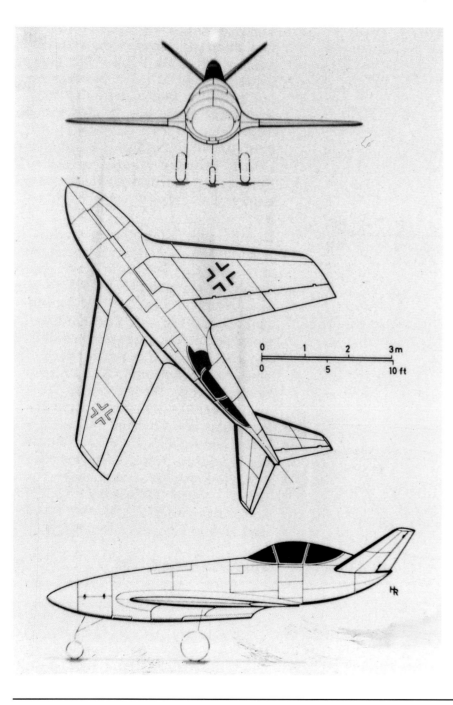

The long nosed Messerschmitt Me P.1106 with its butterfly tail and featuring its starboard side. It was to have been powered by a single Heinkel-*Hirth HeS 011* turbojet providing 2,866 pounds [1,300 kilograms] of thrust. Scale model and photograph by *Dan Johnson*.

What is this? A machine reminiscent of the long-nosed Me 209 V1? Here we have a pen and ink drawing of the proposed single turbojet powered Messerschmitt Me P.1106 from September/October 1944. It featured an extremely long nose which housed a fuel tank large enough to keep it airborne for 60 minutes. Aft of the fuel tank was the cockpit and just forward of the butterfly tail assembly.

The rear starboard side of the proposed long nosed Me P.1106. Woldemar Vogit, Messerschmitt AG's brilliant aircraft designer, submitted this proposed idea to the RLM in response to their call for a fighter with long duration and range. *Vogit* said that in order to get the range and duration it would require a lot of fuel. The only place where a lot of fuel could be carried without affecting the aerodynamics of the machine was to design a long nosed version of their 1939 *Me 209 V1* and fill it completely with a fuel tank. Scale model and photograph by *Dan Johnson*.

Opposite: A pen and ink drawing of a proposed fighter derived from the Me 209 V4 and known as the Me 209 V14. Nothing ever came of this fighter version. Redrawn from the original Messerschmitt AG drawings by *Günter Sengfelder*.

The judges at the RLM didn't like the proposed long nosed Me P.1106 much. According to the judges, placing the cockpit so far aft severely restricted the pilot's forward view. In addition, whenever the pilot looked down, whether to port or starboard, all he was likely to see was the wing. Scale model and photograph by *Dan Johnson*.

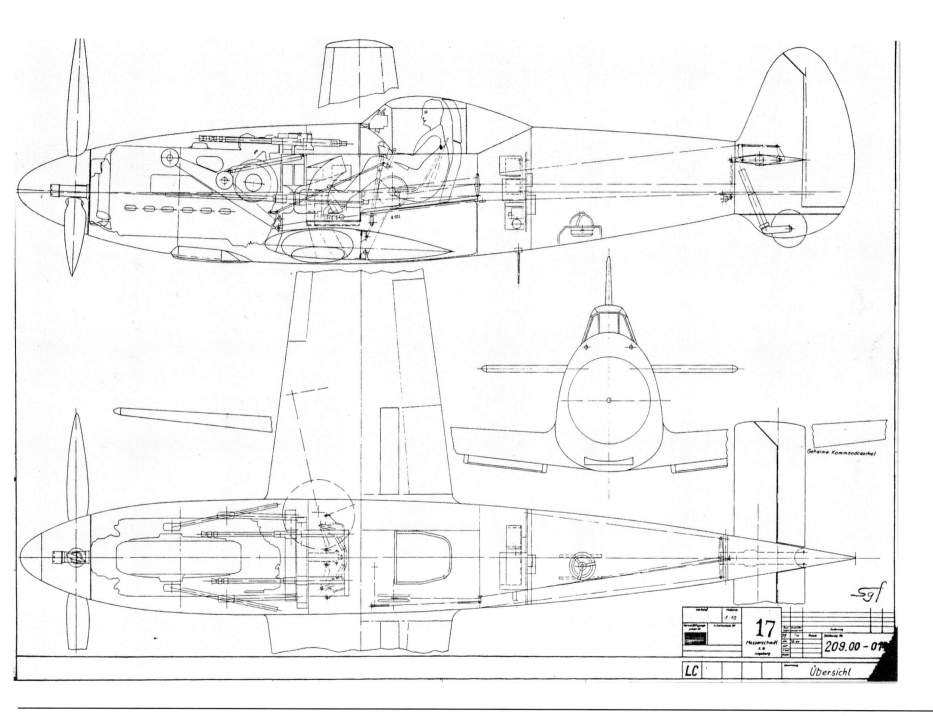

Geheime Kommandosachel

	1:10	**17**	
		Messerschmitt A.G. Augsburg	**209.00-01**
LC			Übersicht

Darryl Greenamyer, the California Lockheed test pilot who flew his highly modified Grumman F8F-2 "Bearcat" faster than Messerschmitt AG's thirty year old FAI Absolute Land Air Speed Record. Greenamyer's air speed on 16 August 1969 was 482.462 mph [776.449 km/h].

A ground level nose starboard side view of Darryl Greenamyer's F8F-2 "Bearcat" nicknamed "#1."

A port side view of Darryl Greenamyer's Grumman F8F-2 "*Bearcat*" coded *NIIIIL*, *#121646*, and nicknamed "*#1.*" It is shown here at Edwards Air Force Base, California.

On 14 August 1979, pilot/owner Steve Hinton flew his highly modified North American P-51 "Mustang," with its contra-rotating propellers, coded N7715C, #44-84961*A*, and nicknamed the "*Red Baron*" to a new *FAI* Absolute World Air Speed Record of 499.059 mph [803.152 km/h] at Tonopah, Nevada.

Steve Hinton's "Red Baron" North American *P-51 "Mustang"* with a single four-bladed propeller before he modified it to carry contra-rotating propellers.